UNIVERSITY OF NORTH CAROLINA
STUDIES IN THE ROMANCE LANGUAGES AND LITERATURES
Number 119

I0660982

CAMUS' HELLENIC SOURCES

CAMUS' HELLENIC SOURCES

BY

PAUL ARCHAMBAULT

CHAPEL HILL

THE UNIVERSITY OF NORTH CAROLINA PRESS

DEPÓSITO LEGAL: V. 2.590 - 1972

ARTES GRÁFICAS SOLER, S. A. - JÁVEA, 28 - VALENCIA (8) - 1972

For M.-H., *intimior intimo meo.*

TABLE OF CONTENTS

FOREWORD

Albert Camus considered himself a son of Greece. His frequent references to Greek myth, his love of sunshine and seashore, his paeans to nature, his fondness for tanned bodies and the silhouettes of young athletes racing along Mediterranean landscapes — these were references, tastes, and inclinations he considered characteristically Greek and pagan. "The world wherein I feel most at home," he wrote in his *Notebooks,* "is the world of Greek myth." [1]

This essay is not an attempt to study Camus' rapport with the Hellenic mind in such a popular, somewhat vulgar light. Indeed, none of the tastes or inclinations mentioned above are specifically Greek: they might just as accurately be referred to as "Polynesian." In the following pages, I have asked myself very specific, very "academic" questions about Camus' alleged Hellenism. Granted that he loved Greece, a land he visited on two occasions, what did he mean by being "a son of Greece"? By having a "Greek heart"? What did he know about Greek culture? From what sources did he draw his information?

Such questions might seem to betray an idle or pedantic curiosity. Academic critics and literary historians are well known for their morbid love of dissection and analysis: their interests often remind one of Bergson's "dead butterflies," pinned, pale and lifeless, to the botanist's board. Of course there is no necessary connection between being a son of Greece and knowing all there is to know about Greek literature. To absorb any culture means, surely, to *feel* what people of that culture feel, or have felt. Who has failed to experience that magic moment in one's identification with a foreign culture when one begins to sense that one's intuitions, one's feelings, one's way of reacting to the

---

[1] A. Camus, *Carnets,* vol. II (Paris, 1964), p. 317.

world are very much like those of the people in the country in which one happens to be. Must that magic moment of total identification with a foreign culture not be preceded, however, by an arduous (if pleasant) intellectual effort? Has one not been obliged to *learn* the language, the literature, the history of the culture he has come to *love?*

Camus' spiritual affiliation to Greece has never been seriously questioned; nor has the real content of his Greek culture been seriously evaluated. One takes him at his word when he declares that he has a "Greek heart," though it hardly seems to occur to critics that quality of feeling is very much a product of quality of understanding. If it is true, as Aristotle and Aquinas have said, that no love is possible without prior knowledge, it seems reasonable to assume that Camus' knowledge of Greek culture is a fair stick wherewith to measure the quality of his love, inasmuch as love can be measured.

This particular facet of Camus' work has been explored in curiously little detail. There have been brief studies dealing with isolated features of Camus' Hellenophilia, or of his classical sources... and the list of titles is rapidly exhausted. [2] I know of only one general attempt to evaluate the depth and the influence of Camus' Hellenic sources on his literary production, and it is totally inadequate. [3]

---

[2] Henri Peyre, "Camus the Pagan," *Yale French Studies,* Spring 1960, no. 25, pp. 20-25; Simone Fraisse, "De Lucrèce à Camus, ou les contradictions de la révolte," *Esprit,* March 1959, no. 3, pp. 437-53; Robert Champigny, *Sur un héros païen,* Paris, 1959; Jacques Hardré, "Camus' Thoughts on Christian Metaphysics and Neoplatonism," *Studies in Philology,* vol. LXIV, 1967, pp. 97-108. To this list might be added an article on Camus' use of Suetonius by Walter Strauss, "Albert Camus' *Caligula*: Ancient Sources and Modern Parallels," *Comparative Literature,* Spring 1951, vol. III, no. 2, pp. 160-173. André Nicolas' study of Camus, *Albert Camus ou le Vrai Prométhée* (Paris, 1966), is organized according to several major Greek myths, but it is not a study of Camus' use of Greek sources.

[3] Dimitri Papamalamis, *Albert Camus et la pensée grecque,* Nancy, 1964. This is a *diplôme d'etudes superieures,* written with enthusiasm, but too hastily compiled, too fragmentary, too uncritical. Papamalamis admits to not having read *Métaphysique chrétienne et Néoplatonisme,* Camus' philosophical thesis at the University of Algiers. No general study of Camus' Hellenic sources can exclude this early essay, which has recently been edited in the "Pléiade" edition of Albert Camus' *Essais* (Paris, Gallimard, 1965, pp. 1224-1313.) A young Italian scholar, Francesco Lazzari, has recently attempted to evaluate the essay ("Metaphysica cristiana e neoplatonismo in un saggio giovanile di Camus," *Revista di Studi Crociani,* vol. 5, April-June 1968,

A reader might legitimately ask whether the presence of the word "Hellenic" in my title is not a misnomer, as this essay covers "Hellenic" phenomena as disparate as Presocratic philosophy, Gnosticism, and Augustinian thought. I am evidently not using the word "Hellenic" in a restrictive sense, to mean Greek culture prior to Alexander's conquests. I am, rather, using it throughout my essay in the broad sense which Camus gives it in *Christian Metaphysics* and other essays, meaning not only Greek culture before the Hellenistic age, but the totality of Mediterranean culture that was in any way affected or influenced by classical Greece, up to and including Augustine. For a Camus (as we shall soon discover), the term "Hellenism" did include works as chronologically and spiritually disparate as the *Odyssey*, the *De Rerum Natura*, the *Enneads*, the *Confessions*, even Gnostic literature. The Alexandrine writings of Philo and Plotinus, the early Christian treatises of Justin and Clement, even the treatises of Valentinus and Basilides — they all perpetuate, at least in part, what Camus considered as "Hellenic" attitudes towards the world, however transformed or distorted these attitudes may have been.

I have approached Camus' "Hellenic" sources, roughly speaking, in chronological order. Such an arrangement is obviously not intended to suggest that Camus was influenced by classical Greece, by Christianity, by Gnosticism and by Augustinism in successive periods of his life. Camus' attitudes towards Hellenism (and indeed Christianity) underwent no perceptible evolution during his literary career, except in certain isolated cases — his conception of Plotinus' doctrine, for example — which I shall touch upon. There might, as I have indicated in my essay, have been some progress or development in Camus' use of his sources. Taken on the whole, however, Hellenism and Christianity (as well as other related terms) meant much the same to him in 1960 as in 1936. Indeed, the kernel of his thinking on these matters had, I believe, already taken shape in the mid- and late thirties. I therefore do not thinking it misleading to place side by side, let us say, what Camus says about the Prometheus myth in 1936, and what he says in 1956. If there is a change of attitudes, I have not failed to underline it.

---

pp. 228-41); but his article demonstrates little except the fact that Lazzari could not have read more than the first ten pages of Camus' essay.

My point of reference, however, has constantly remained the historical sources themselves, rather than Camus' own works. Why is this so? As I reread Albert Camus' works with the present subject in mind, it became progressively clear that he constantly referred to Hellenism either as a historical phenomenon that is separate from Christianity, or in its relation to and contrast with Christianity. I therefore sensed that two initial chapters needed to be written, the first of which would clarify Camus' vision of classical Greece and his use of classical Greek sources, the second of which would evaluate his attitudes towards the historical fusion of Hellenism and Christianity, and the consequences of this fusion. Moreover, in his early essay on *Christian Metaphysics*, Camus himself had remarked that the encounter of Greek and Christian ideas had engendered two other autonomous systems of thought, Gnosticism and Augustinism, the latter being the final illustration of Hellenized Christianity and marking the official end of the "Hellenic era." Chapter three is, consequently, an attempt to detect not only the obvious but the hidden presence of Gnosticism in Camus' major works; and chapter four is a roughly similar search for the presence of Augustine. Such is the way I have decided to organize the present essay, without in any way pretending to have been exhaustive.

The limits of the essay should be made clear from the outset. This is not, strictly speaking, an essay in criticism, but an exploration of classical literary sources, their acquisition, their uses, their misuses, and their transformations. This is not a stylistic study, nor is it an attempt to uncover the more subtle relationships between Camus' sources and his creative talent. Finally, I am not attempting to infer from Camus' scholarly or historical lapses that he was a second-rate writer. There may, however, be some conclusions to be drawn about his status as a *penseur*. Hopefully this essay may enlighten and inform those who, like myself, have long admired the "passionate monotony" of Camus' pen, and long entertained some doubts about the substantive value and the historical accuracy of his ideas on Hellenism and Christianity.

I have quoted Camus or his sources in the original text only when my purpose has been to infer verbal resemblances. In all other cases I have quoted in English. Whenever possible, I have consulted the same editions as those used by Camus himself. This procedure holds not only for such specialized studies on Hellenism and early Christian

literature as those of Emile Bréhier, Alfred Loisy, Pierre de Labriolle, and others, but even for general works such as Boris Schloezer's translations of Chestov, or Geneviève Bianquis' translations of
Nietzsche. The reader should not be overly shocked, therefore, to find
me referring to a French translation of *The Birth of Tragedy,* as it
was the precise source Camus used.

Debts of gratitude are the only debts that scholars are pleased
and willing to acknowledge. It is a pleasure to extend my deepest
thanks to the following institutions and persons, without whose help
this essay could literally not have been written: the National Foun-
dation on the Arts and the Humanities, for a Younger Scholar
Fellowship which allowed me to write the better part of this essay
during the spring semester of 1969; Professor Myron Lichtblau,
Dean Prucha, Dr. John C. Honey, and the trustees of Syracuse University, for a grant-in-aid towards its publication; Professors Henri
Peyre, Jeffery Carre, and Daniel Poirion, for their unfailing friendship
and encouragement; R. P. Georges Folliet and R. P. Goulven Madec,
of the editorial staff of *Etudes Augustiniennes,* Paris, for many hospi-
table hours spent in their library, and for their innumerable ideas and
suggestions, especially during the preparation of Chapter Four. The
initial version of this chapter appeared in *Recherches Augustiniennes,*
1969, under the title "Augustin et Camus."

SYRACUSE, NEW YORK
July, 1971

Chapter I

CLASSICAL SOURCES

A. Homer

The Homeric heroes whose names appear most consistently in Camus' literary production are: Sisyphus, Achilles, and Ulysses.

"According to Homer, Sisyphus was the wisest and the most prudent of mortals. According to another tradition, however, he had an inclination for the trade of bandit. I fail to see any contradiction." [1] These are the witty opening lines of the final section of Camus' essay on Sisyphus. The reader is immediately led to believe that Camus is alluding to Odysseus' description of Sisyphus' punishment, in Book XI of the *Odyssey*, as well as other unspecified Greek texts; and it comes as something of a surprise to discover that he derived all of his information, and much of his phraseology, from two banal schoolboy sources. A collation of Camus' text, in the original, with each of these sources, in turn, illustrates how clever Camus can be at transforming textbook prose into attractive literature:

A. Camus, *Le Mythe de Sisyphe,* in *Essais,* Paris, 1965.	P. Commelin, *Nouvelle Mythologie des Grecs et des Latins,* Paris, 1907.
"Si l'on en *croit Homère,* Sisyphe *était le plus sage et le plus prudent des mortels.*"	"*C'était* aussi, *dit Homère, le plus sage et le plus prudent des mortels.*"

---

[1] A. Camus, "Le Mythe de Sisyphe," in *Essais* (Paris, 1965), p. 195. "Le Mythe..." will henceforth be referred to as *MS*.

"Selon une *autre* tradition cependant, il inclinait au métier de *brigand*."

"*D'autres* enfin ... ont dit qu'il exerçait toutes sortes de *brigandages* ...."

"Les dieux avaient *condamné* Sisyphe *à rouler sans cesse* un *rocher jusqu'au sommet d'une montagne* d'où la pierre retombait *par son propre poids*."

... les poétes prétendent qu'il est *condamné à rouler incessamment* une *grosse roche jusqu'au haut d'une montagne*; parvenue au sommet, la roche descend aussitôt *par son propre poids*."

"*Il livra leurs secrets* [i.e. des dieux]. *Egine, fille d'Asope, fut enlevée par Jupiter*. Le père s'étonna de cette disparition et s'en *plaignit à Sisyphe*. Lui, qui *avait connaissance de l'enlèvement*, offrit à Asope de l'en instruire, à la condition qu'il donnerait de l'eau à la citadelle de Corinthe. Aux foudres célestes, il préféra la bénédiction de l'eau. *Il en fut puni dans les enfers*. (p. 195.)

"Il aurait ... *révélé le secret* des dieux. *Jupiter* ayant *enlevé Egine*, fille du fleuve *Asopus*, celui-ce s'adressa à Sisyphe pour savoir ce qu'était devenue sa fille; Sisyphe, *qui avait connaissance de l'enlèvement*, promit à Asopus de l'en instruire, à condition qu'il donnerait de l'eau à la citadelle de Corinthe. Sisyphe ... en fut puni dans les Enfers ...." (pp. 238-9.)

The second paragraph reproduces a substantial part of the information on Sisyphus contained in the *Grand Dictionnaire Universel*:

Camus, *Ibid.*, p. 195.

Grand Dictionnaire Universel, art. "Sisyphe"

"On dit encore que *Sisyphe étant près de mourir* voulut imprudemment éprouver l'amour de sa femme. Il lui *ordonna de jeter son corps sans sépulture au milieu de la place publique*. Sisyphe se retrouva dans les enfers. Et là, irrité d'une obéissance si contraire à l'amour humain, *il obtint de Pluton la permission de retourner sur la terre pour châtier sa femme. Mais quand il eut de nouveau* revu le visage de ce monde, goûté l'eau et le soleil, les pierres chaudes et la mer, *il ne voulut plus retourner dans l'ombre infernale* .... *Bien des années* encore, il

"*Sisyphe étant près de mourir* ... ordonna à sa femme de jeter son corps au milieu de la place, sans sépulture; ce quelle exécuta ponctuellement. Sisyphe, l'ayant appris *dans les enfers*, trouva fort mauvais que sa femme eût obéi si fidèlement à un ordre qu'il ne lui avait donné qu'afin d'éprouver son amour pour lui. *Il demanda à Pluton la permission de retourner sur la terre*, uniquement *pour châtier sa femme* de sa dureté. *Mais quand il eut de nouveau* respiré l'air *de ce monde, il ne voulut plus* retourner en l'autre, jusqu'à ce qu'après *bien des an-*

vécut devant la courbe du golfe, la mer éclatante et les sourires de la terre. Il fallut un arrêt des dieux. *Mercure vint saisir l'audacieux par le collet* et, l'ôtant à ses joies, *le ramena de force aux enfers* où son rocher était tout prêt." (p. 195.)

nées Mercure, en exécution d'un arrêt des dieux, *le saisit au collet et le ramena de force aux enfers,* où il fut puni pour avoir manqué à la parole qu'il avait donnée à Pluton . . . ."

Germaine Brée quite correctly points out that "there are, in reality, two images of Sisyphus," and that these are a little hard to reconcile. "There is the Sisyphus, who, having returned from Hades, lives in the glory of the sun and the sea, knowing that he can temporarily defy the gods; his rock is then simply his knowledge that he is mortal and must die. But there is also the Sisyphus who is condemned for all eternity to his desperate task. Rather surprisingly it is on this second Sisyphus that Camus focuses our attention, holding him up as a symbol of the happiness available to man." [2]

Miss Brée's remark is most interesting in the light of Camus' sources. The two images of Sisyphus correspond, in fact, to two separate source books; and Camus is indicating that even the suffering Sisyphus, the "Homeric" Sisyphus, who is a more fitting model for modern man, can be happy. It seems doubtful, however, whether Camus had any specific Homeric text in mind when he spoke of the Sisyphus "according to Homer." Homer did call Sisyphus "the most clever of men," but not "the most wise and prudent of men." [3] (The Homeric epithet, being morally neutral, seems to mitigate the injustice of Sisyphus' punishment at the hands of the gods.) Nowhere does Homer pretend that Sisyphus had "put death in chains." Camus' Sisyphus is the product of two banal sources, transformed by the magic wand of artistry. "Myths," argued the author of *The Myth of Sisyphus,* "are made so that the [poetic] imagination can give them life." [4] In asserting his originality, Camus was surely being faithful to Homer, in a deeper sense of the word.

Other works of Camus' bear out irrefutably that he had, at some time, read the Homeric epics with a passionate interest. He seemed

---

[2] G. Brée, *Camus* (New York, 1964), p. 207.

[3] Homère, *Iliade,* ed. and trans. P. Mazon, I (Paris, 1949), Bk. VI, 11. 152-54.

[4] *MS,* in *Essais,* p. 196.

most responsive to Books XVIII, XXII, and XXIV of the *Iliad*, particularly to the episode of Achilles' return to battle after the death of Patroclus. The *Notebooks* of March 1942 indicate that he was reading or rereading the *Iliad* during that period: "Patroclus' horses weeping in the battle because their master is dead. And (Book 18) Achilles' three great cries as he returns to the battle, encamped on the last ditch, fearsome in his gleaming armour. And the Trojans retreat." [5]

In *The Exile of Helen,* the same epic gesture becomes the symbol of a defiant challenge to a "dreary and disincarnate" modern world, which threatens to wipe out all the ancient virtues, and particularly that of friendship. [6] In *The Rebel*, Achilles' vengeance illustrates the Greek sense of moral restraint: the warrior's imprecations against heaven never degenerate into vindictiveness or blasphemy. [7] Indeed, Achilles is a credible and human hero only because he can temper his terrible wrath with a virile pity. His slaughter of Hector in Book XXII would leave a most bitter impression were it not tempered by the tears of Book XXIV: "Book 24. Achilles' grief as he weeps in the night after the victory. Priam: 'For I have brought myself to do a thing that no one else on earth has done — I have raised to my lips the hands of the man who killed my sons.' " [8] "The greatest praise," Camus concludes, "that one can shed on the *Iliad* is that, even though we know how the war will end, we still share the anguish of the Greeks as the Trojans drive them back to the ships .... How thrilling it must have been for people hearing the story for the first time!" [9]

As the meaning of the *Iliad* is centered, in Camus' mind, about the drama of Achilles, the "whole meaning" of the *Odyssey* is epitomized by Ulysses' rejection of Calypso's offer of immortality. [10] Such is the paradoxical greatness of Homer's heroes: their deeds while in battle merely underscore the grandeur and the beauty of everyday life. On Achilles' shield, one remembers, are engraved not merely scenes of valor but accounts of commonplace human activity. [11]

---

[5] A. Camus, *Carnets,* trans. P. Thody (London, 1964), vol. 2, p. 3.

[6] A. Camus, "L'Exil d'Hélène," in *Essais,* pp. 856-57.

[7] A. Camus, *L'Homme révolté,* henceforth *HR*, in *Essais,* p. 439.

[8] A. Camus, *Carnets,* trans. P. Thody, vol. 2, p. 3.

[9] *Ibid.,* pp. 3-4.

[10] *Ibid.,* p. 7.

[11] *Iliad*, XVIII, 468-617.

In this mortal life, where every second counts, who is to say whether plowing, hunting, and dancing are any less important than war? Surely this was one of the Homeric "messages" to which Camus was most responsive. In Homer no detail of reality is relegated to the shadows; every episode, as Erich Auerbach so convincingly demonstrated in his *Mimesis,* chapter one, is endowed with dramatic relief. Argus' recognition of his master is as filled with suspense as the slaughter of the suitors is filled with cruelty; and the solemnity of Ulysses' tour of the underworld does not prevent Agamemnon from advising him "never [to] be too gentle with your wife nor show her all that is in your mind." [12] Homer's Ulysses, in short, like Camus' Rebel, "refuses divinity in order to share the struggles and the destiny of every man." The world of light "remains his first and his last love." [13]

B. *Aeschylus*

Camus' adaptation of the *Prometheus Bound* was one of the first plays performed by his *théâtre du travail* in 1937. [14] Even as a young playwright he responded symbiotically to the essentially "grave" character of Aeschylus' theatre, which he thought illustrative of those rare epochs of history when love of life and metaphysical despair coexist. [15] Aeschylus (a veteran of two wars, like some of our own European and American writers) wrote during one of those periods of history which Camus was fond of calling literary *charnières* (hinges), when life is filled both with danger and glory, when the future is uncertain and the present dramatic. [16] At the core of his own dramatic production, Camus glimpsed "the same inexhaustible and enigmatic sun as that which shines through the desperate but optimistic production of Aeschylus." At the center of the Aeschylean universe, there lies,

---

12 A. Camus, *Carnets,* trans. P. Thody, vol. 2, p. 7.

13 *HR,* in *Essais,* p. 708: "Nous choisirons Ithaque, la terre fidèle.... Dans la lumière, le monde reste notre premier et notre dernier amour."

14 The play was first performed by that troupe on March 7, 1937. (A. Camus, *Théâtre, Récits, Nouvelles,* henceforth *TRN,* Paris, 1962, p. 1689.)

15 *TRN,* p. 1690: "Le Théâtre de l'Equipe... se tournera... vers les époques où l'amour de la vie se mêlait au désespoir de vivre."

16 *Ibid.,* p. 1699: "Eschyle est le combattant de deux guerres." Cf. *Carnets,* II, p. 248: "A Athènes, le spectacle est une chose grave."

"not a meagre absurdity, but an enigma, a meaning which is badly deciphered only because it is blinding." [17]

Historically, Camus situated Aeschylus' tragedies "close to the religious and dionysiac origins of tragedy." Hence, the confrontation between two almost equally powerful forces: on the one hand, man and his need for self-assertion, on the other the divine forces of the cosmos. [18] Aeschylus being an essentially religious figure (Camus agreed on this point with Professor Georges Méautis, perhaps his main source of information on Aeschylean theatre), [19] the balance of forces, in Aeschylus' plays, is always slightly "tilted" in favor of the divine principle. The *Prometheus* trilogy, in its original sense, is a history of the development of divine Justice: Prometheus and Zeus are reconciled, in the final play, both having grown in wisdom. [20]

Nietzsche had called the *Prometheus Bound* "the most sublime poem in the history of civilization." [21] Camus, hardly less laudatory, called it the very "archetype" of Greek tragedy. [22] No myth can fairly be said to have obsessed him more than that of the Fire-Bearer. Like Nietzsche, he realized that the Prometheus legend is a "revolutionary ideal." [23] Modern Western civilization, he reflects, has adopted the Promethean myth as its most faithful reflection. Our age likes to call itself "Promethean." But are we the faithful sons of Prometheus? Such is the question raised by *Prometheus in Hell,* an essay published in 1952, and by some remarks in *The Rebel.* [24]

In the early Greek theogonies, Camus argues, Prometheus was chained to a pillar, an eternal martyr whom Zeus eternally refuses to pardon. Aeschylus increased the hero's stature, made of him a lucid enemy of the gods, and, in the first part of the trilogy, at least, a victim of injustice.

---

[17] "L'Enigme," in *Essais,* p. 865: "Eschyle est souvent désespérant; pourtant, il rayonne et réchauffe. Au centre de son univers, ce n'est pas le maigre non-sens que nous trouvons, mais l'énigme, c'est-à-dire un sens qu'on déchiffre mal parce qu'il éblouit...."

[18] "L'Avenir de la Tragédie," in *TRN,* pp. 1704-05.

[19] G. Méautis, *Eschyle et la Trilogie,* Neuchâtel, 1936. Camus quotes this source in *Carnets,* I, p. 237.

[20] "L'Avenir de la Tragédie," in *TRN,* pp. 1704-05.

[21] F. Nietzsche, *Humain, Trop Humain,* in *Œuvres,* vol. I (Paris, 1918), p. 419.

[22] See footnote 20.

[23] *Carnets,* I, p. 174.

[24] *HR,* in *Essais,* pp. 438-39; cf. "Prométhée aux Enfers," in *Essais,* pp. 839-44.

Metaphysical revolt was, therefore, not an unfamiliar concept to the Greeks, and Prometheus remained, at least until Euripides, one of its most celebrated heroes. The Greeks, however, never stretched their sense of revolt to the point where it would embrace their entire pantheon, or the cosmos itself. ("The Greeks," Camus was fond of repeating, "never exaggerated anything.")

The Aeschylean Prometheus does not rebel against all of Creation, but against Zeus alone, who is, after all, but one of the gods. Neither Prometheus nor Zeus is entirely justified, neither is the sole depository of justice. The story of Prometheus' struggle against Zeus must not be interpreted as a struggle of good against evil. Each of the protagonists, morally speaking, is composed of light and darkness, innocence and guilt. [25]

It might be assumed that Prometheus is the best model of twentieth-century revolutionary activity, and that the protest raised thousands of years ago in the Scythian wastes has reached its climax in the unprecedented historical convulsion of our time. Something tells us, however, that this victim continues to be persecuted among us, and that we are as ever deaf to the great cry of human rebellion of which he is the solitary herald. [26] Neither the Marxist convulsion nor the Industrial revolution, which in the past century and a half have shaken our universe to its foundations, can rightfully claim Prometheus as a model. Men today continue to suffer in prodigious numbers on the narrow surface of the globe. They are deprived of fire and food. Freedom, to them, is a luxury that can wait. But Prometheus is a hero that so loved manking as to give him both fire and freedom, technology and art. Modern man needs and worries about technology alone. He holds art and what art implies as an obstacle and a sign of bondage. What characterized Prometheus, quite to the contrary, was that he could not separate art from the machine. He believed it possible to liberate the body and the soul at the same time. Contemporary man thinks it necessary first to liberate the body, even if the soul must die a temporary death. But can the soul die a temporary death? If Prometheus were to come back, he would be nailed to his rock, in the same of the very humanism which he ini-

---

[25] *HR, in Essais,* pp. 438-39.
[26] "Prométhée aux Enfers," in *Essais,* p. 841.

tially symbolized. He would be insulted by the same hostile voices that echo in the play of Aeschylus: Fire and Violence. [27]

Modern man is therefore not entitled to consider the myth of Prometheus as his own. In our time the Promethean myth has been abused. Modern revolutionaries have set the Promethean drama in the sterile plain of history rather than in the natural setting of the rugged Caucasus. Prometheus has become a Caesar, a Procurator, a Grand Inquisitor. He sows fire among men, but he has not restored man's freedom, like the figure in Aeschylus. He has introduced technology, but he has neglected the arts. The Marxist Prometheus, like his Capitalist counterpart, has accomplished one half of his revolution, and in so doing, he has merely deepened the misery of those he was supposed to save. [28]

Is it possible to revolt against one's condition and to save mankind at the same time, Camus asks? One can easily imagine Prometheus' reply to this question: "Mortals, I promise you reform and reparation if you are clever enough, virtuous enough, strong enough to achieve them with your own hands." Prometheus knew that he would suffer in the name of justice; but could he foresee that his Myth would be so distorted, and that the absolute Justice for which he suffered would be replaced by the monumental mockery of "historical justice"?

Camus' conclusion is categorical: if the myth of Prometheus is to be truly beneficent for mankind, it must be restored to its original meaning. "Myths have no life of their own. They await an incarnation. Let one man in this world answer their appeal, they offer us their power intact. This is one myth we must preserve. We must see to it that its sleep is not mortal, so that it can rise again. ... If we must resign ourselves to living without beauty, and the freedom of which beauty is a sign, the myth of Prometheus is there to remind us that any mutilation of man can only be temporary, and that no part of man is served if he is not served in his entirety." [29]

Camus' attempt to defend the myth of Prometheus against its modern distortions can only elicit admiration. It is difficult to imagine a more perceptive analysis of modern titanism, in both its Capitalist and Marxist versions, than his *Prometheus in Hell*, nor is it

---

[27] *Ibid.*

[28] *HR*, in *Essais*, p. 647; cf. *Ibid.*, p. 703: "Prométhée a-t-il jamais eu cette face d'ilote ou de procureur?"

[29] "Prométhée aux Enfers," in *Essais*, pp. 843-44.

easy to debase a myth more than the Promethean myth has been debased in the name of "dynamic idealism."

Camus' evident purpose in writing *Prometheus in Hell* was to restore the true, i.e. Aeschylean, sense of the myth. His reader is left wondering, however, whether his own conception of the Greek myth was unobstructedly clear, and whether he was not to a certain extent the victim of his hasty readings. His knowledge of the *Prometheus* legend seems to have been derived from three main sources: he had, of course, been deeply influenced by the *Birth of Tragedy*; he was familiar with Professor Paul Mazon's translation of the *Prometheus Bound*; and he was occasionally swayed by Professor G. Méautis' book on Aeschylus, which compensates in scholarly solidity for what it lacks in Nietzschean flamboyance.

This plurality of sources perhaps accounts for some of the confusions, not to say contradictions, which I have encountered in my attempt to reconstitute Camus' remarks about the Prometheus legend. One of Professor Méautis' main theses is that Aeschylus is an essentially religious figure, and that he can be understood only by those who attempt to measure the depth of his religious ideals. [30] Nietzsche, on the other hand, considers Prometheus a rebel who wrested civilization from the hands of the savage gods and forced them to create an alliance with him: the wisdom he has acquired places the existence of the gods and their laws under his *control*. [31] Mazon, finally, thinks it erroneous to consider Prometheus as a rebel in any sense. The Athenian spectator knew that, at the end of the final play of the trilogy, Zeus and Prometheus were to be reconciled and equally honored on Athenian altars. Each new presentation of the Promethean trilogy reminded him of the immemorial truth that Zeus had become a God of Justice only after long centuries of conflict. His initial violences had long retarded the reign of peace. Only with clemency had he been able to obtain the allegiance of his arch-rival, Prometheus. Only with time had Zeus brought peace to Olympus. [32]

Each of the essays wherein Camus discusses the myth of Prometheus seems dominated by one of these points of view, to the partial

---

[30] G. Méautis, *Eschyle et la Trilogie*, p. 50.

[31] F. Nietzsche, *La Naissance de la Tragédie*, trans. G. Bianquis, Paris, 1949.

[32] P. Mazon, ed., *Eschyle*, I (Paris, 1941), p. 153.

or total exclusion of the others. In *Prometheus in Hell,* the perspective is clearly a Nietzschean one: Prometheus is featured as a rebel against the gods ("ce révolté contre les dieux") who brought down to earth the symbolic fire of *art* and *technique.* In *The Rebel,* while suggesting that the Prometheus legend is "the greatest myth of rebellious intelligence," Camus agrees with P. Mazon that it is not to be interpreted as a revolt against all creation, nor even against all divinity, but as a private settling of accounts between a god and a demi-god. In *The Future of Tragedy,* finally, Camus echoes G. Méautis' opinion that the dramas of Aeschylus were essentially religious. Never does Camus seem to arrive at a proper synthesis of these opinions; indeed, perhaps such a synthesis would be impossible, for though the interpretations of Mazon and Méautis hardly differ, it would take a certain amount of mental agility to reconcile them with Nietzsche's.

A curious feature of Camus' essays on the Prometheus myth is that while attempting to salvage the original spirit of the play and the legend, he was erroneous in the details. It is clear, for example, that Camus consulted Mazon's edition and translation of the *Prometheus Bound,* particularly while writing those pages of *The Rebel* that pertain to Prometheus. Some of the quotations he attributes to Prometheus are taken literally from Mazon's translation, for instance: "J'ai délivré les hommes de l'obsession de la mort ... j'ai installé en eux les aveugles espoirs." [33] The following textual collation also seems to indicate that Camus' interpretation of the Prometheus legend, in *The Rebel,* is a faithful reflection of Paul Mazon's critical ideas:

A. Camus, *L'Homme Révolté,* in *Essais,* Paris, 1965.	P. Mazon, ed., *Echyle,* Tome I, Paris, 1941.
"Les premières théogonies nous montrent Prométhée enchaîné à une colonne, sur les confins du monde, martyr éternel exclu à jamais d'un pardon qu'il refuse de solliciter." (p. 43.)	" ... les premiers auteurs de *Théogonies* le représentaient enchaîné à une colonne a l'extrémité du monde, martyr éternel à qui nul pardon n'était jamais accordé." (p. 153.)

---

[33] *HR,* p. 438; cf. P. Mazon, ed., *Eschyle,* I, *Prométhée enchaîné,* ll. 248-50.

One looks in vain, however, for a certain number of other lines which Camus purportedly "quoted" from the play. Where, for example, in the dialogue between Hermes and Prometheus (*Prometheus Bound*, lines 944-1092) did Camus find the following dialogue? " 'O Justice, my mother,' cries Prometheus, 'you see what I am being made to suffer.' And Hermes rails at the hero: 'I am astonished that, being a soothsayer, you did not foresee the torture that you would undergo.' 'I knew it,' replies the rebel." [34] Despite its insertion in quotation marks, this "Aeschylean" fragment is entirely the product of Camus' imagination, the nearest equivalent to it in Aeschylus being Prometheus' cry, in the closing lines, "O majesty of my Mother, and thou, Ether, who dost make the light offered to all men to roll around the world, can you not see the iniquities I must endure?" [35] When these lines are uttered, however, Hermes has left the stage, and Prometheus is alone. [36]

C. *Sophocles*

Camus' veneration for Sophocles — the word is hardly an exaggeration — should in itself be proof sufficient that he never allowed himself to be hypnotized by Nietzsche's ideas on Greek tragedy. For Nietzsche, the Aeschylus of the early period, "prior to the influence of Sophocles," represents the culmination of Greek tragedy. Sophocles already marks the beginning of a decline. "We must acknowledge," Nietzsche argued with ironic serenity, "that the most beautiful characters in Sophoclean theatre — an Antigone, an Electra, an Oedipus — sometimes reason with an intolerable vulgarity." Nietzsche found it hard to tolerate Sophocles' attempts to transfigure suffering into sanctification, as well as his resignation to the "immeasurable distance" which separates the human order from the divine. [37]

---

[34] "Prométhée aux Enfers," in *Essais*, p. 843.

[35] P. Mazon, *op. cit.*, ll. 1090-92.

[36] Had Camus read any other Aeschylean plays? One finds in his *Notebooks* a fragment from *Les Perses* (I, 233), and a description of Helen (II, 198) attributed to Aeschylus: "Ame sereine comme le calme des mers, beauté qui ornait la plus riche parure, doux yeux qui perçaient à l'égal d'un trait, fleur d'amour fatale aux cœurs." The reference is to the Agamemnon, ll. 739-44.

[37] F. Nietzsche, "Socrate et la Tragédie," in *La Naissance de la Tragédie*, trans. by G. Bianquis (Gallimard, 1949), p. 165.

Indebted as he was to Nietzsche for so many of his attitudes towards Greek culture, Camus did not share his distaste for Sophocles, whom he called "the greatest tragic playwright of all time." [38] A necessary ingredient of tragedy, he argued in *The Future of Tragedy,* is equilibrium between individual assertiveness and cosmic forces; and in Sophocles, the equilibrium reaches its point of perfection. Man, with his desire for self-assertion, is locked in an eternal struggle against the forces of the cosmos. Neither camp is ever "favored," neither ever "yields." In this sense, Sophocles is more humanistic than Aeschylus who, being closer to the religious origins of tragedy, tilts the balance slightly in favor of the cosmic forces. [39]

Though Camus' works contain occasional references to *Antigone,* the two Oedipus plays are the only works of Sophocles that he comments in any significant detail. The Oedipus myth is referred to as early as the *Notebooks* of August, 1939: "1) Oedipus suppresses the Sphinx and, if he dissipates mysteries, it is by his knowledge of man. The whole Greek universe is clear. 2) But this is the same man whom destiny savagely tears apart, implacable in its blind destiny. Clarity without shadow of the tragic and the perishable." [40]

In *The Myth of Sisyphus,* Oedipus is represented as an absurd hero, whose tragedy begins when he knows the full truth about himself. At that moment of lucidity, blind and desperate, he realizes that the only bond that links him to this world is the fresh hand of a young girl. It is then, Camus observes, "that he utters an immoderate thought: 'Despite so many trials, my advanced age and the greatness of my soul allow me to judge that all is well.' " [41] Sophocles' Oedipus thus expresses the victory of absurdity. His final words "echo in the savage and limited universe of man. They teach us that all [the possibilities] are not, have not been, exhausted. They chase from this world a god who had entered with dissatisfaction and the taste

---

[38] "L'Avenir de la Tragédie," in *Essais,* p. 1705.

[39] *Ibid.*

[40] *Carnets,* I, pp. 161-2.

[41] *MS,* in *Essais,* p. 197. Camus seems to be adopting Leconte de Lisle's translation, *Oidipous à Kolonos,* in *Sophocle* (Paris, 1899), p. 139: "car mes misères, le long temps et ma grandeur d'âme me font trouver que tout est bien." But these words are uttered not "at the very moment" when Oedipus' tragic destiny is revealed to him, but many years later. Nowhere is Oedipus ever "reconciled to his destiny."

for useless suffering. They make of destiny a man's business which must be settled among men." [42]

In *The Rebel*, Oedipus is depicted as a model of "limited revolt." Not presuming to be innocent (for he, too, is part of destiny), he complains but never pronounces "the irreparable words." Though blind and miserable, he realizes that "all is well." [43]

Camus' extreme latitude with the detail of the Sophoclean text perhaps serves to explain his occasional infidelity to its spirit. Is it fair to make of Sophocles' Oedipus a hero of the absurd? Does Oedipus not discover the truth about himself, and does the revelation of his tragic destiny not endow his universe with a meaning, however terrible? Oedipus' moment of intensest suffering coincides with the illuminating realization that "now, at last, *everything can be explained.*" His attitude towards destiny, in the *Oedipus at Colonus*, is far different from that described in *The Myth*. Far from chasing a "god of suffering" from this world and making of destiny a man's busines, Oedipus bestows a final blessing upon Colonus and Athens. Of the gods, he says that "their eyes can discover, even long after the deed, those who, in contempt of heaven, have turned towards madness." [44] After advising Theseus, King of Athens, "never to become one of these," he advances towards the sacred grove wherein he is to die, "led by Hermes the guide and the nether goddess." [45] Camus' interpretation, particularly in the *Myth*, is unfortunately distorted by a curious need to endow the Sophoclean gods with a taste for blood.

His interpretation given the Oedipus myth in *The Rebel* is no more consonant than that in the *Myth*. In an astonishing shift of perspective, Camus there depicts an Oedipus "who knows he is not innocent," who realizes that he must "not pronounce the irreparable words of revolt." But the paradox of the Oedipus plays is that Sophocles intended neither to debunk the gods nor to pronounce Oedipus guilty! In both plays, destiny is a divine affair and continues to be so until the final chorus. The same Apollo who had foretold the sufferings of Oedipus predicts that he will be a benefactor to the city

---

[42] *HR,* in *Essais*, p. 438.

[43] *MS,* in *Essais*, p. 197.

[44] *Oedipus at Colonus*, ll. 1536-37 (my translation). Cf. Leconte de Lisle, *Sophocle*, p. 217.

[45] *Ibid.*, ll. 1547-48. Cf. Leconte de Lisle, *op. cit.*, p. 217

that will give him shelter. [46] Oedipus never denies, particularly in the *Colonus,* that the gods govern human affairs: "Never has an impious man, that I know of, ever escaped the gods," he tells the Chorus. [47] "Whether things turn this way or that," declares Polynices, "depends on the gods." [48] "Our promise [to respect the grave of Oedipus]," declares Theseus in the closing lines, "has been heard by our protecting genius [of Colonus] and by Horcus, Son of Zeus." [49] In fairness to Sophocles, it cannot be said that he ever makes of destiny "an affair to be settled among men."

Yet, paradoxically, Oedipus never considers himself "justly punished by the gods." In neither play does he admit that he is unconsciously or even partially guilty. On the contrary, the old man of Colonus is quite sensitive to any implication that he was responsible for his crime. "I *endured* the crime, strangers, quite despite myself, may God be my witness. Nothing in all of this was *voluntary.*" [50] When Creon tries to prove that he is guilty, Oedipus retorts: "You pour upon me murders, marriages, and misfortunes of all kinds, which I endured, alas, despite myself." [51]

The most authentic interpretation of Sophocles is contained in *The Future of Tragedy* (1955). It is reasonable to suppose that that perceptive essay had been preceded by a more painstaking reading of Sophocles than that which had preceded the *Myth* and *The Rebel.* In this essay, Camus suggests that Sophoclean tragedy is characterized by a perfect equilibrium of forces: on the one hand, an assertion of faith in the justice of the gods, and a corresponding declaration of faith in man, the most wonderful of the world's innumerable wonders. The gods are not to be justified at the expense of man's legitimate effort to control and understand his destiny. Neither man nor the cosmic (and social) powers are to be considered entirely innocent or entirely guilty. "Antigone is right, but Creon is not wrong." In Sophocles' "perfect" tragedies, the tension between individual and

---

[46] *Ibid.,* ll. 85-93. Cf. Leconte de Lisle, *op. cit.,* p. 145.

[47] *Ibid.,* ll. 275-81. Cf. Leconte de Lisle, *op. cit.,* p. 154.

[48] *Ibid.,* ll. 1443-46. Cf. Leconte de Lisle, *op. cit.,* p. 212.

[49] *Ibid.,* ll. 1766-77. Theseus thus reaffirms the sacred character of Oedipus' place of burial, consecrated by an oath made to the protecting *daimon* of Colonus and to Horcus. Cf. Leconte de Lisle, *op. cit.,* p. 227.

[50] *Ibid.,* ll. 521-23. Cf. Leconte de Lisle, *op. cit.,* p. 168.

[51] *Ibid.,* ll. 962-64. Cf. Leconte de Lisle, *op. cit.,* pp. 193-94.

cosmic powers is never resolved. The hero rebels against the cosmic order that oppresses him; but his rebellion is an implicit assertion of the existence and the value of that order. In Sophocles it is the presence of an opposite force that buttressnes the other and enables each force to define itself. Oedipus could not be Oedipus without the oracle; but the oracle would not make any sense if Oedipus did not attempt to resist it. [52]

Judging by the number of times they are quoted or otherwise referred to, Homer, Aeschylus, and Sophocles would seem to have been Camus' major poetic sources. Of course he occasionally quoted from other Greek poets (Pindar, Euripides), and alluded to other myths (Eurydice, the Minotaur). Frequently enough, however, the poetic quotations are so well known — a certain text from Pindar's *Third Pythian,* for example, somewhat overused by French authors since Valéry — that their presence need not lead one to assume that Camus had read the author's works; and the myths sometimes have such a plurality of sources (including the most banal dictionary articles) that it need not be supposed that Camus had gathered it from its original Greek source. Many a former student of college Greek would be more than a little embarrassed were he asked to submit a bibliography of the Greek works he has read in their entirety, even in translation. Every humanist, for example — and Camus was no exception — remembers having read somewhere during his college days that a Greek poet once said: "Whom the gods love dies young." It need not be taken for granted, however, that whoever uses that cliché has read the fragments of Menander. [53]

One might none the less have expected Euripides, that irreverent despiser of Olympian cant, to receive more attention from Camus than he did. One wonders why he is so rarely and briefly quoted. The *Notebooks* of 1941 contain a quotation, allegedly taken from *Iphigenia in Tauris,* which is decidedly Euripidean in tone: "Now is the time to prove by our acts that the dignity of man is in no way inferior to the grandeur of the gods." [54] And the epigraph to the essay, "Return to Tipasa," written in 1953, is taken from a chorus in *Medea:*

---

[52] "L'Avenir de la Tragédie," *TRN,* pp. 1703-05.

[53] Camus quotes that proverb in *MS,* (*Essais,* p. 145). Cf. Menander, *Dis Exapaton,* l. 13.

[54] *Carnets,* I, p. 235. I have been unable to locate this text in *Iphigenia in Tauris.*

"You have sailed with a furious spirit far from your father's house, you have passed through the sea's rocky straits, and now you live in a foreign land." [55] In *The Future of Tragedy*, finally, Camus reiterates Nietzsche's condemnation of Euripides' "decadent" dramas. [56] Euripides fails to provide him that "Grèce de l'ombre, pessimiste, sourde, et tragique," which he loved so much, and his excessive rationalizing deters from the true spirit of tragedy. [57] Tragedies can thrive neither in the hothouse of unconditional faith nor in the ice of atheistic scientism. And Euripides, because he "tips the scales of tragedy in favor of the individual and of psychology, proclaims an individualistic drama," which amounts to nothing less than decadence. In the Euripidean dramas, as twenty centuries later in those of Racine, "the tragic genre culminates in a perfection characteristic of chamber music." [58]

It is, then, perhaps Nietzsche's hostility to Euripides, as well as Camus' temperamental distaste for some of the rationalism in the age of the Sophists that accounts for his apparent reserve towards Euripides, whose relative absence on Camus' poetic shelf remains conspicuous.

---

[55] "Retour à Tipasa," in *Essais*, p. 867. The reference is to *Medea*, ll. 431-35.

[56] "L'Avenir de la Tragédie," in *Essais*, p. 1706.

[57] *Métaphysique Chrétienne...*, in *Essais*, p. 1309.

[58] "L'Avenir de la Tragédie," in *Essais*, p. 1706. Euripides himself must have detested the clever sophistry of his day, to judge from the way he deploys it in his characters' speeches.

Like Nietzsche, to whom he perhaps owed his predilection for the Presocratics, Camus wondered whether the "eternal principle" is not to be found at the source of Western philosophy.[1] Must the philosopher not begin, like Empedocles, by offering his heart "openly to the grave, suffering earth, and, in the sacred night, promise to love it faithfully and fearlessly until death with its heavy burden of fatality, and to despise none of its enigmas?"[2] Such was the greatest contribution of the Presocratics:

> [they] suppressed final causes, but kept intact the eternity of the principle which they imagined. Only undirected force is eternal, the Heracleitean "Game" ["Jeu"]. The world is eternal because it is gratuitous. Hence art, and art alone, being equally gratuitous, is capable of apprehending this force. No judgment can account for the universe, but art can teach one to repeat it, as the universe repeats itself in its eternal cycles. On the same strands, the primordial sea tirelessly repeats the same words and turns up the same creatures, astonished to be alive. To say "yes" to the world, to repeat it, is to recreate both the world and oneself. It is to become the great artist, the Creator.... The "grave and suffering earth" is the only truth. It is the sole divinity. Like Empedocles, who plunged into Etna to find [the] truth where it is, in the womb of the earth, Nietzsche invites man to

---

[1] A. Camus, HR, in Essais, p. 482: "Nietzsche retourne aux origines de la pensée, aux présocratiques." Cf. F. Nietzsche, La Naissance de la Philosophie, trans. by G. Bianquis (Paris, 1938), p. 18.

[2] HR, in Essais, p. 411 (Camus' epigraph to HR, from Hölderlin's Death of Empedocles). Cf. Carnets, II, p. 316.

lose himself in the cosmos in order to rediscover his eternal divinity and to become his own Dionysus. [3]

True wisdom, that "sagesse aux yeux pleins de larmes," of which René Char spoke, is to be found in the molten center of the earth. [4]

A passage like the foregoing indicates to what extent Camus' attitude toward Presocratic philosophy was conditioned by Nietzsche's interpretation of that period. Camus uses precisely the same words to describe Nietzsche's philosophical mission as Nietzsche does to describe that of Heracleitus: "[démontrer] la présence de la loi dans le devenir et *du jeu dans la nécessité*." [5] Camus' use of the word "jeu" to describe the "eternal, undirected force" of Heracleitus, is also derived from a French translation of Nietzsche: "If one were to pose the following problem to Heracleitus: why isn't fire always fire? Why is it sometimes water, sometimes earth?, he would answer simply: 'It's a game; do not take it tragically, and especially do not make it a moral problem.' " [6]

Might not Camus have found the concept of "jeu" in Heracleitus' fragments? True, Heracleitus does employ the image of "children's games" (πάιδων 'αθύρματα) in one of his fragments. [7] But there is no evidence of Camus' ever having read the fragments of Heracleitus; and, even if he had, it is doubtful whether they would have enabled him, or anyone else, to reconstitute unaided, a philosophical system which, even to Heracleitus' contemporaries, was notorious for its obscurity. The description of the theory of Becoming as a Heracleitean "game" is a Nietzschean invention so fictitious that one wonders

---

[3] *Ibid.*, p. 484. Cf. *Essais*, p. 1424: "Héraclite et Nietzsche, tous les deux persuadés que la vie est un jeu."

[4] "René Char," in *Essais*, p. 1164: "Char revendique avec raison l'optimisme de la Grèce présocratique. ... Ce que Char appelle 'la sagesse aux yeux pleins de larmes' revit ici, à la hauteur même de nos désastres."

[5] *HR*, in *Essais*, pp. 482-83. F. Nietzsche (*La Naissance de la Philosophie*, trans. by G. Biaquis, p. 741) describes Heracleitus' mission in exactly the same terms: "contempler la présence de la loi dans le devenir et du jeu dans la nécessité."

[6] F. Nietzsche, *La Naissance de la Philosophie* (trans. by G. Bianquis), p. 70.

[7] H. Diels, *Fragmente der Vorsokratiker* (Berlin, 1951), fr. 70, p. 167.

whether Nietzsche is not confusing Heracleitus either with Schopenhauer or with himself. [8]

Camus' portrait of Empedocles is also the product of a highly
romantic vision, which owes more to Hölderlin and Nietzsche than to
historical reality. Hölderlin's Empedocles "offers his heart openly
to the grave, suffering earth, and promises to love it faithfully and
fearlessly until death, with its heavy burden of fatality, and to despise
none of its enigmas." [9] Nietzsche's Empedocles is the very epitome
of the tragic hero, who plunges into the volcano in order to know
the universe's secrets. Only an insatiable "Apollonian instinct" like
that of Empedocles can compel nature to create ever new worlds of
art and knowledge. [10] Camus' Empedocles, like Nietzsche's, is a Presocratic Faust.

Camus voices other opinions on Presocratic philosophy, principally
when he discusses the problem of Being and Becoming in terms of
the conflict between Nature and History. It is impossible, he argues,
to deny the existence of Being unless one chooses to qualify as absurd
our need for irrefutable knowledge, and our "nostalgie de la fixité."
It is, on the other hand, impossible to deny the existence of Becoming
without betraying one's perceptions.

One need uphold neither the immobility nor the eternal mobility
of Zeno's arrow: "Being cannot be said to exist exclusively in the
realm of essence. Where can essence be grasped, unless it be on
the level of existence and Becoming? It cannot be said, on the other
hand, that Being is nothing but existence. Perpetual Becoming cannot
exist: a beginning is necessary to all things. Being cannot be experienced except in Becoming; Becoming is nothing without Being. The
world is not frozen in a fixed structure, nor is it merely in motion.
It is both movement and fixity. The dialectic of history, for example,
is not racing indefinitely toward an unknown goal. It centers about
a central point of reference, which is "limit". Heracleitus, the inventor of Becoming, nevertheless set bounds to this perpetual stream,

---

[8] Ch. Andler, *Nietzsche, sa vie et sa pensée*, III, p. 107, quoted in
F. Nietzsche, *La Naissance de la Philosophie*, trans. by G. Bianquis, p. 8:
"Quand il [Nietzsche] parle d'Héraclite et Empédocle, c'est Nietzsche qu'il
faut entendre."

[9] *HR*, in *Essais*, p. 411.

[10] F. Nietzsche, "La Tragédie et les Esprits Libres," (lecture delivered
Sept. 22, 1870), in *La Naissance de la Tragédie*, trans. by G. Bianquis (Paris,
1949), pp. 190-91.

symbolized by Nemesis, the goddess of "limits," who was so fatal to her transgressors. Any system of thought that presumes to explain the contradictions of modern revolt might do well to turn to this goddess for inspiration." [11]

Being cannot be negated unless one wishes to describe one's need for rational stability as senseless, nor can Becoming be denied unless one wishes to deny one's sense experience. Camus appeals, here again, to Heracleitus in order to resolve the apparent contradiction between Being and Becoming. One wonders, however, whether in this passage Camus is being entirely faithful to Nietzsche's conception of Heracleitus. According to Nietzsche, Heracleitus thought of Being as an "empty fiction:" the world of appearances is the only world, which is not to be contrasted with a "real world." [12]

Nietzsche's interpretation of Heracleitus goes contrary to that of two other Hellenists, Emile Bréhier and Jean Grenier, whose influence on Camus should not be underestimated. According to Bréhier, the Heracleitean universe is composed of two seemingly opposite principles, unity and perpetual flux. Being is to be found within Becoming: there is a primordial law, a *logos*, hidden in the depths of nature. Concealed from vulgar mortals, it is like the gold one discovers after sifting great masses of earth, or like the truths of Apollo, wrapped in enigmatic utterances. The Heracleitean *logos*, according to Bréhier, is more accessible to intuition than to tradition. [13] Jean Grenier's interpretation of Heracleitus' system is quite similar: Heracleitus, he says, insists on the spectacle of universal flux, in order to underscore the eternal Essence which is the common substratum of all the superficial contradictions. Heracleitus mocks those who simultaneously worship Dionysus and Hades, only that they might realize that the god of joy and the god of sadness alike are but illusory masks of the same God, who is One. [14]

---

[11] *HR*, in *Essais*, p. 699.

[12] F. Nietzsche, "Extrait d'Ecce Homo," in *La Naissance de la Tragédie*, trans. by G. Bianquis, pp. 144-45: "l'affirmation du dualisme et de la guerre, du devenir, à l'exclusion radicale du concept même de l'être," as well as the doctrine of the Eternal Return, had, according to Nietzsche, been taught by Heracleitus. Cf. F. Nietzsche, *La Naissance de la Philosophie*, trans. by Bianquis, p. 23 (a translation of *Goetzendaemmerung, Die Vernunft der Philosophie*, no. 2).

[13] E. Bréhier, *Histoire de la Philosophie*, vol. I (Paris, 1938), pp. 57-58.

[14] Jean Grenier, *Essai sur l'Esprit d'Orthodoxie*, (Paris, 1938), p. 143.

As in the case of Aeschylus, Camus' opinions on Heracleitus are a composite of his various and often divergent sources. His solution of the problem of Being and Becoming, like his attempt to resolve the apparent contradiction between Nature and History, owes much to the interpretations of Heracleitus by Bréhier and Grenier, perhaps more than they do to the interpretation by Nietzsche. According to Nietzsche, the Heracleitean *logos* is the eternal "game," *perceived by the philosopher's intuition,* which proclaims that unity and substance are illusory, and that being is an empty fiction. Bréhier, on the other hand, calls this logos a "primordial substance," and Grenier goes so far as to identify this substance with "Being" and "God." [15] It would appear, therefore, that Camus' understanding of the notion of Heracleitean fixity owes more to the opinions of Grenier and Bréhier than to those of Nietzsche.

Camus appeals to the Presocratics in order to resolve certain fundamental linguistic problems, such as the nature of language and the interrelation between language and concepts. He realized that the problem of language is not unrelated to that of Being and Becoming. If the universe is in perpetual flux, then the words used to designate things must be reduced to ephemeral signs. Their significance changes, as it were, with the passing of each second. Words become like dead leaves, swept along by the current of Becoming. As the leaf is never quite the same at the second turning of the stream as it was at the first, so the word "man," uttered today, does not mean what it meant yesterday. In short, if all is Becoming, word and concept are one and the same. Both are a mere *flatus vocis,* infinitely variable in their significance. If, on the other hand, the universe is both Being and Becoming, the word, as exterior sign of the signified concept, can vary, while the concept remains a static entity.

Camus attacks this problem head on, as is his custom. Like Nietzsche, he believes that knowledge is incompatible with a universe in perpetual flux: "To live in Becoming is to abandon all hope of knowledge." If a spoken word designated nothing but a state of Becoming, any so-called knowledge of the world would be reducible to a momentary observation of its passing appearances. Literature would, accordingly, be possible, but science would not. If, on the other hand,

---

[15] *Ibid.*

the spoken word invariably designates nothing except Being, it creates an entire logical system that appears like the product of a dream or the cruel diversion of a prisoner trying to occupy his solitude. [16]

Like the Presocratics, Camus does not hesitate to profess his faith in the possiblility of knowledge:

> The Presocratics described an immobile and transparent universe, wherein every object corresponded to an expression. They did not balk at the consequences of this initial affirmation. For if every word is, at it were, "guaranteed" by an object in the world, then nothing can be negated, and Protagoras is right in proclaiming that all is true. Science is equivalent to sensation, and dialogue is impossible. The world contains no objections. To tell the truth, all one need do is speak. But then Gorgias is equally entitled to assert that all is false, since there are, in fact, more objects in reality than words to designate them. No word can give a complete account of that which it designates, nothing can be demonstrated, since nothing can be exhausted.... Greek thought oscillated for a long time between these extreme conclusions, and it is not a coincidence that it found its purest literary form in the dialogue, as if, throughout the history of Hellenic thought, Protagoras and Gorgias would, for centuries, vie tirelessly with each other. [17]

Camus thus admits that the Presocratics did not resolve the epistemological problems posed by Being and Becoming. They must be credited, however, attacking the problem courageously, and for elucidating the difficulties. [18]

In the final analysis, Camus felt drawn to the Presocratics for intuitive and emotional rather than academic reasons. Like them, he experienced that nostalgia for a secret Unity. In this world of a thousand faces, the Presocratics looked for "eternal relations that might sum them up, and sum themselves up, in a single principle." [19] They hungered for the "beatitude of the mind, compared to which

---

[16] "Sur une Philosophie de l'Expression," *Essais*, p. 1674.

[17] *Ibid.*, p. 1675.

[18] *Ibid.*, p. 1676: "la théorie des Idées marque la victoire des mots plus généraux que les objets et plus près de la patrie idéale dont ce monde n'est qu'une copie délavée."

[19] *MS*, in *Essais*, p. 110. Cf. E. Bréhier, *op. cit.*, p. 63, for an excellent summary of Parmenidean thought.

the myth of the blessed in heaven is a ludicrous travesty." But they, too, could not be satisfied by facile solutions. A nostalgia for Unity, a hunger for the absolute, he says, echoing Chestov's opinion on Parmenides, illustrates the essential orientation of the human drama. [20] The fact that this nostalgia exists does not imply that it must be immediately or remotely appeased: "For if, breaching the gap that separates desire from conquest, we affirm, along with Parmenides that the One (whatever it may be) is real, we are faced with the ridiculous contradiction of a mind asserting the Unity of the whole and demonstrating by that very assertion its own difference from the whole and the diversity which it claimed to resolve. This new vicious circle is enough to crush our hopes." [21] In short Camus, like Chestov, denies Parmenides' assertion that thought and being are identical and that reality imposes a constraining necessity on human reason.

A reconstitution of Camus' opinions on the Presocratics is about as challenging as a reconstitution of Presocratic thought itself, for in both cases the texts are fragmentary. Camus' analysis of the Presocratics is marred by two major weaknesses: he relies far too much on Nietzsche, and he assumes that Presocratic philosophy constitutes a single philosophical tradition. To suggest that they "suppressed final causes," is both anachronistic and inexact. The concept of finality was not developed by the Presocratics; and it is not at all certain whether they were concerned, as Camus claims (in the wake of Hölderlin and Nietzsche) with finding the primordial substance of the universe. Aristotle was the first to make such a claim about the purpose of the Presocratics' investigations, but Aristotle, after all, read the Presocratics with a specific question in mind: "What is the primordial matter of the universe?" Thus formulated, the question is Aristotle's, not the Presocratics'; and no one has ever proved that Heracleitus, Parmenides, or Empedocles were in fact preoccupied by the problems which one inevitably attempts to resolve when reading them. [22] What is indisputable is that the philosophic orientation represented by Anaximenes, Anaximander, Heracleitus, and other "physicists" is

---

[20] L. Chestov, *Le Pouvoir des Clefs*, trans. by B. Schloezer (Paris, 1927), p. 248: "Parménide croit que la pensée et l'être sont identiques. Je crois, moi, qu'il n'en est rien...; dans le domaine métaphysique il n'y a pas de vérités certaines."

[21] *MS*, in *Essais*, p. 110.

[22] On this point, see E. Bréhier, *op. cit.*, p. 42.

directly opposed to that represented by the Pythagoreans and by Parmenides. There are, according to Emile Bréhier, two major currents of Presocratic philosophy: on the one hand Ionian positivism, which is intuitive, experimental, unmathematical, hostile to myth, religious tradition, and initiation cults; on the other hand, the rationalism of Parmenides and Pythagoras, which attempts to construct reality by means of reflection, is principally dialectical, hostile to experimentation, and receptive to mythology and to the problem of human destiny. [23] Camus takes into account none of the differences, basic or superficial, which make of the Presocratic philosophy a variegated and elusive period of history. His remarks on the Presocratics are both interesting and intelligent, they reveal insights into Camus' own mind, but their historical imprecision endows them with little objective value.

* * *

With the exception of Plotinus, Camus does not seem interested by post-Socratic philosophy. He was, to a large extent, hypnotized by the Nietzschean thesis that Socrates' radical separation of dialectical reason and artistic intuition was the undoing of both Greek philosophy and literature. Plato does not occupy an important place in Camus's work. He is credited with having resolved the problems posed by the relation of language to reality and given Greek thought its purest literary form, the dialogue. Camus repeats Brice Parain's opinion that "the *Dialogues* are nothing but a long combat between language and reality, wherein, paradoxically, language has the upper hand." The theory of Ideas, according to Camus, marks a decisive moment in the history of the problem of language: words win the battle over objects, since they are more general, and nearer the ideal realm, of which this world is nothing but a faded copy. If words are to have meaning, this meaning must come from a source other than the world of sense, so fleeting as it is and subject to change. This other source, which so many Greek minds aspired to with all their hearts, is Being. Plato's solution is not psychological, but cosmological. He made of language an intermediary in the hierarchy which stretches from Matter

---

[23] *Ibid.*, p. 65.

to the One. The *logos* is a genus of Being, one of the spheres of universal harmony: compared to it, this world is unimportant. [24]

Camus could not possibly find in Platonic thought a confirmation of his most personal convictions. His tragic love for the world of sense experience could not harmonize with a system that considers the sense world "like the faded copy of a masterpiece." Being a moralist more than a metaphysician, Camus might, conceivably, have been attracted by the moral "consequences" of Platonic thought — its asceticism, for example, and its love of beauty — but the Platonic cosmology, the Platonic epistemology, orientated towards a source of Being beyond the senses, could at best elicit from him an affectionate indifference. As a verbal artist, Camus considered Plato's hostility to poetry and rhetoric, as well as his relegation of true Beauty to a "world beyond" as inadmissible prejudices. [25] Plato is rarely mentioned, save as the major source of the Socratic doctrine. [26]

Socrates answered better than Plato to Camus' taste for philosophic concreteness. He lived in a period not dissimilar to ours: "There was evil in men's souls because there was contradiction in their speeches. The most commonplace words, laden with a plurality of meanings, were distorted, shorn of the simple usage attributed to them. Such problems cannot leave us indifferent. We, too, have our Sophists, and we stand in need of a Socrates, whose mission was to remedy men's souls by means of an adequate dictionary. If the words justice, beauty, and goodness have no meaning, men are then free to tear

---

[24] "Sur une Philosophie de l'Expression," in *Essais*, pp. 1675-76. Cf. *Carnets*, II, pp. 34-35; B. Parain, *Essai sur le Logos Platonicien* (Paris, 1942), p. 89: "Si le langage est une image du monde sensible, qui émane de lui et participe de sa fluidité perpétuelle, aucune connaissance n'est possible. Le seul salut serait donc de rompre avec le langage pour chercher ailleurs la réalité essentielle." (Parain is quoting Socrates in the *Cratylus*.)

[25] *HR*, in *Essais*, p. 657: "On observa pourtant l'hostilité à l'art qu'ont montrée tous les réformateurs révolutionnaires. Platon est encore modéré. Il ne met en question que la fonction menteuse du langage et n'exile de sa république que les poètes. Pour le reste, il a mis la beauté au-dessus du monde."

[26] Except for Socrates, and the Dialogues wherein he is the presiding figure, Camus' references to Plato are exceedingly sparse. In *The Rebel*, Camus evokes the figure of Callicles, who, in the *Gorgias*, attemps to demonstrate that the supreme law of Nature is force. Callicles' apology of immoralism (*akolasía*) is subsequently refuted by Socrates. (*HR*, in *Essais*, p. 439. Callicles the immoralist is, in Camus' words, a "préfiguration du type vulgaire du nietzchéen." Cf. Plato, *Gorgias*, 484 a.)

one another apart. Socrates' attempt — and failure — was to *endow* words with an irreproachable sense; having failed in this he chose to die." [27] Camus, echoing an opinion of Brice Parain, describes Socrates' philosophic mission as a "search for the law that transcends our acts and our expressions." One cannot be sure of the nature of Socrates' conclusions to the problem of language. One does know that he died for speaking his mind unequivocally, which is perhaps the best indication that he considered the problem of language in moral rather than epistemological terms. The martyr of the *Phaedo* realized that obscure and ambiguous language is both unfavorable to philosophy and damaging to the soul. [28]

Camus shared to a certain extent what Nietzsche contemptuously described as Socrates' moral optimism: his predilection for self-knowledge, his indifference to the natural sciences, his faith in reason tempered by an honest evaluation of reason's limitations. [29] His scepticism, however, was far more radical. Notwithstanding his profession to know nothing, Socrates managed to demonstrate that he knew a respectable number of things: more, in fact, than any of his interlocutors. "Know thyself" was, for Socrates, a philosophical rule of thumb. For Camus it is an impossible ideal:

> Of whom and of what can I say: "I know that." I can feel this heart within me and I assume that it exists. I can touch the world about me, and again I judge that it exists. There ends my knowledge. All the rest is construction. For if I attempt to grasp the "I" of which I am sure, if I attempt to define and summarize it, it becomes like water flowing through my fingers. I can delineate all the successive faces this "I" can assume, and all the faces it has assumed, as well as my education, my upbringing, my ardor or my silences, my grandeur or my baseness. But faces cannot be added up. This very heart of mine will forever remain undefinable. Between the certitude that I exist, and the content I endeavor to give this certitude, the breach will never be closed. I shall always be a stranger to myself. In psychology, as in logic, there are several truths, but there is no one truth. The "know thyself" of Socrates is about as valuable as the "be virtuous" of our confessionals. They reveal both

---

[27] "Sur une Philosophie de l'Expression," in *Essais*, pp. 1673-74.
[28] *Ibid.*, p. 1675.
[29] *MS*, in *Essais*, p. 111.

a nostalgia and an ignorance. These are sterile games played with great subjects. [30]

Camus, in sum, adopts the Socratic method in order to arrive at more modest conclusions than its inventor. The supreme virtue of Socratism is that it forces one to know the limitations of one's mind. Its illusion (as Nietzsche warned so eloquently) is that it sheds a false clarity on things that should remain wrapped in mystery. So-cratic serenity, Camus warns, can easily become a "paresse du coeur." [31] Socrates illustrates, par excellence, one dimension of the Hellenic ideal, its taste for order, measure, reason, and light. His weakness, however, resides in his insensitivity to the mute and pessimistic Greece of which Nietzsche spoke with such eloquence. Socrates' professed distaste for the tragic poets (with the symptomatic exception of Euri-pides) is, in effect, a betrayal of his principal weakness. [32]

Camus, like Nietzsche, criticized the false serenity of Socratism, while admiring the person of Socrates: "When Nietzsche accused Socrates of being the gravedigger of ancient tragedy, he was, in a certain sense, correct ... in the same sense as Descartes can be said to mark the death of the tragic movement born with the Renaissance. During the Renaissance period, in fact, the traditional Christian universe was brought into question by the Reformation, the discovery of a new world, and the growth of the scientific spirit. The individual slowly asserted himself in the face of religion and destiny . . . ." [33]

Socrates thus remains an ambiguous symbol. He was responsible, on the one hand, for bringing order and meaning to a civilization beset by linguistic and conceptual chaos; but the "enlightenment of the mind" that he epitomizes can obscure the dark face of truth. When Socratism serves the false *clarté* of the salons, when it constructs rather than frees the bloodstream of philosophy, art, and life, its dangers must be loyally denounced. The fate of Socrates has, however, resembled the swing of a pendulum. While understanding Nietzsche's reasons for denouncing the illusory Socratism of nineteenth-century

---

[30] *Ibid.*: "Le 'connais-toi toi même' de Socrate a autant de valeur que le 'sois vertueux' de nos confessionaux. Ils révèlent une nostalgie en même temps qu'une ignorance. Ce sont des jeux stériles sur de grands sujets."

[31] *Métaphysique Chrétienne*, in *Essais*, p. 1309.

[32] "L'Avenir de la Tragédie," in *TRN*, p. 1700.

[33] *Ibid.*, p. 1706.

art and science, twentieth-century man must rehabilitate the Socratic symbol, now submerged by a morass of movements and ideologies. The movement of liberation that began with the Renaissance is drawing to a close to the deafening music of military drums and mass slogans. Everywhere one turns, Socrates is gagged, vilified, and assassinated. Our is the century of petty thinkers and great demagogues. Socrates is proven wrong by being put to death, "the most current sort of refutation employed by our contemporary political society." [34] A great and unequal combat is being waged between the forces of terror and the forces of dialogue. Socrates is no longer surrounded and adulated — he is dying in his prison cell, tragically alone. [35]

The error of Socratism resides, therefore, not in the truths it proclaims, but in those it excludes. Nietzsche thought it necessary to attack Socrates and Christianity with powerful arguments. But in our day, it is imperative that we defend Socrates, or at least what he represents, since our era threatens to replace him with values that are the very negation of all culture. Nietzsche would here risk obtaining an undesired victory. Every error, Camus was fond of repeating, is the result of an exclusion. The error of Socrates was his suppression of intuition, art, and irrationality. The tragic error of today is that Socrates has been put to death. [36]

* * *

Camus rarely devotes his attention to Greek philosophy after Socrates. The period between Plato and the Patristic era is represented at best by occasional fragments of Aristotle, taken from secondary sources, or by allusions to the Cynics, the Stoics, the Epicureans. Nothing seems to indicate that Camus had anything but a passing acquaintance with Greek thought between the death of Plato and the Christian era. [37]

---

[34] "La patrie mondiale," (Dec., 1948), in *Essais*, p. 1587.

[35] *Actuelles*, I, in *Essais*, p. 375.

[36] *Carnets*, II, p. 79.

[37] In *MS* (*Essais*, p. 109), Camus quotes at length from Aristotle's *Metaphysics*, IV, viii, 6; but, according to R. Quilliot (*Essais*, p. 1434), Camus had encountered the quotation in Chestov's *Le Pouvoir des Clefs*. There is no clear indication that Camus had ever read Aristotle in the text.

He had most certainly read Epicurus in translation (J. Grenier, *Albert Camus*, p. 65), and he discusses some of Epicurus' ideas in *HR, Essais*, pp. 440-43).

Plotinus is a noteworthy exception. In chapter three of *Christian Metaphysics*, Camus considered his system as a bridge between Hellenic philosophy and Christian gospels. Plotinus is the Greek thinker who allowed Augustine to transform Christianity into a teachable metaphysics. He endowed Christian thought, not with a doctrine, but with a method and a way of looking at reality. [38] Camus considers the system of Plotinus in the light of the religious and mystical aspirations that were characteristic of his period. Despite his bent for mysticism and irrationality, Plotinus had a "Socratic taste" for explaining the universe rationally. In this respect, his "personal tragedy" anticipates the drama of Christian metaphysics. For Plotinus, a rational knowledge of the Good coincides with a solution to the problem of the soul's destiny. In his system, as in psychoanalysis, the diagnosis coincides with the treatment. His demonstrations of the existence of the Good are means of ascending towards the Good. Knowledge is a contemplation and a recollection rather than a rational construction. Human reason functions like the sensibility of an artist: "Reality is beautiful, therefore it has an explanation." It is not the world of appearance that Plotinus is interested in, but the reverse side of reality, which Camus calls his "lost paradise."

The thought of Plotinus, Camus argues, seems quite similar to Christianity; yet, the two systems are irreducibly different. Plotinus' world is an eternally harmonious cosmos: all one needs to do is contemplate it. The Christian, by contrast, is engaged in the movement of history. A Christian can, and does, separate truth from beauty, as in the conflict of faith and reason. For Plotinus, the search for Truth coincides with the search for Beauty. [39] Plotinus posits a procession of three hypostases which link the world of sense reality to the highest principle of the universe: the One, the Logos, and the World-Soul. How does Plotinus arrive at a demonstration of their existence? Camus' paraphrase is illuminating:

Epictetus is paraphrased once, in *Actuelles*, II, *Essais*, p. 740, and in *HR*, *Essais*, p. 440. Marcus Aurelius is quoted several times: in *Métaphysique Chrétienne* (*Essais*, p. 1227); *Carnets*, I, p. 252; *HR*, *Essais*, p. 440. Camus also quotes fragments by Antisthenes (*Carnets*, I, p. 251) and Peregrinus Proteus (*MS*, in *Essais*, p. 102).

[38] *Métaphysique Chrétienne*, in *Essais*, pp. 1269-93: "La Raison Mystique."

[39] *Ibid.*, pp. 1269-72.

If the world is beautiful, something must be alive within it, and something must order it. The animating spirit is called the World-Soul. The higher principle which maintains life within preordained boundaries is called Intelligence. The unity of an order, however, must be superior to that order. Thus there exists a third principle above Intelligence, which is the One. Let us reason in reverse. No being can be deprived of its unity. There can be no unity without form, or *logos,* the logos being the very principle of that unity. This is simply another way of stating that there can be no being without soul, since the logos is the necessary act of the soul. The first method of reasoning posits three stages in the explanation of the universe; the second method posits three levels of depth within the Self. Both these methods coincide. Metaphysical reality is nothing other than the spiritual life considered in itself, the first being an object of knowledge, the second of an interior asceticism. A coincidence of objects means a coincidence of methods. The One, the Intelligence, and the World-Soul express the same divinity, the first in its fullness, the other two as in a reflection. The procession of the three hypostases shows how unity and multiplicity can be reconciled. This hypostatic procession, which underlies any rational explanation of the world, finds its human equivalent in conversion, which is a movement of the soul in search of its origins.

The One superabounds and produces the Logos (or Intelligence). From Intelligence, in turn, springs the World-Soul. Thus Intelligence and the World-Soul are at the same time identical with, and distinct from, the One. At their source they are identical with the One as fire is identical with the heat it produces, and a flower with its perfume. Turned towards the lower world, however, the Logos splinters into duality, and the World-Soul into multiplicity. "The One," says Plotinus, "is all things, while being none of these things. It is the principle of all things, since all things, in a sense, return to it, or rather, to its level . . . . " [40]

Camus pursues his analysis with a comparison of Neoplatonism and Christianity. In some respects, he argues, Plotinus differs radically from the Gospels, whereas in others he endows the Christian writers with "a method and an orientation of thought." [41] For Plotinus, a

---

[40] *Ibid.,* pp. 1273-86.
[41] *Ibid.,* p. 1291.

constant "return within oneself" is the necessary condition for the attainment of truth. "God is immanent within us . . . . We bear within us the three hypostases, since it is through interior recollection that we achieve ecstasy and union with the One." [42] For the Christian, on the other hand, truth is revealed from the outside. The Incarnation of God in history was entirely independent of man's desires. For a Neoplatonist like Porphyry, for example, Christianity was an adherence to an exterior and irrational body of truths. [43]

Another difference resides in the privileged position that Christianity grants to man in the cosmos. Christian humanitarianism, that is, the privileged position given to man in the universal scheme, is a repulsive notion to Plotinus' Greek mind: "These people," he says of a group of Christian Gnostics, "do not hesitate to call the basest of men their brothers; but they do not dare thus to name the sun, the stars of heaven, and even the soul of the world, so irrational is their language." [44]

The Christian concept of Creation and the Christian conviction that the world will come to an end conflicts with Plotinus' idea that the world is eternal. Porphyry, Plotinus' disciple, was shocked by the very suggestion that the Creator should ever have been separated from his Creation in an immemorial past, and that He should ever see the Universe disappear from his eternal sight: "So the Creator would see the heavens vanish (can one imagine anything more superbly beautiful than the heavens?) while the rotten bodies of men, once annihilated, would rise again, including those which in life were repulsive and unbearable to the eye?" [45]

Camus' analysis concludes with the idea that, on some points, the thought of Plotinus is consonant with Christianity. The Neoplatonic scheme of Being, he suggests, according to which all forms of existence participate in higher forms, enabled Christianity to resolve the "contradictions" between reason and mysticism, divine immanence and divine transcendence. Plotinus furnished Christianity with a method and an orientation. After him, the fusion of Hellenic metaphysics

---

[42] *Ibid.*, p. 1284.
[43] *Ibid.*, p. 1287.
[44] *Ibid.*
[45] *Ibid.*, p. 1289.

with evangelical faith henceforth seemed possible. The Plotinian principle of participation enabled the theologians of the Council of Nicea to resolve, by means of a vocabulary both subtle and varied, the problems of the Incarnation and of the Trinity. [46] "It is possible," concludes Camus, "to speak of an influence of Neoplatonism on Christian thought. More correctly, it is the influence of a metaphysical doctrine on a religious system . . . . Plotinus can quite rightly be taken as the symbol of this influence. He prepared and molded philosophic formulas which in time were ready to be used [by Christian theologians] . . . . " [47]

Most of Camus' analysis of Plotinus is of merely incidental importance to the Camus reader. It therefore calls for a brief commentary only insofar as several of the major themes of this analysis recur in later works, and under different forms. Camus' analysis of the Plotinian system is generally precise. He is inaccurate, however, in portraying the alleged "opposition" between mysticism and rationalism in Plotinus as a "personal tragedy," which "anticipates the drama of Christian metaphysics." Practically nothing is known of Plotinus' personal life, and there is no evidence of a personal tragedy or of any conflict at all. [48] Camus was excessively fond of dramatizing the "conflicts" that supposedly tear apart those who attempt to conciliate a life of reason with a religious sensibility. To speak of such a conflict between mysticism and reason within a Hellenic soul that was completely foreign to Christianity strikes me as simply anachronistic.

Camus' analysis of the difference between Plotinus and Christian thought is ambiguous. He attributes far too much importance to Plotinus' diatribe against a mysterious group of Christian Gnostics (in *Enneads*, II, 9), as if Plotinus' objections to Gnosticism necessarily prefigured what his objections to Christianity *might* have been. [49] There is in fact no allusion to Christianity in any of Plotinus' writings. The unknown and heretical character of the Gnostic sect to which Plotinus addressed his grievances allows one to doubt whether the same objections might in turn be applied to Christianity. [50]

---

[46] *Ibid.*, p. 1291.

[47] *Ibid.*, p. 1293.

[48] Pierre Hadot, *Plotin ou la Simplicité du Regard* (Plon, 1963), p. 11: "Que savons-nous de Plotin? Quelques détails, finalement peu de chose."

[49] *Métaphisique Chrétienne* . . . , in *Essais*, pp. 1286-88.

[50] *Ibid.*, p. 1286.

The greatest inaccuracies of Camus' analysis occur in a section entitled "Meaning and Influence of Neoplatonism." [51] His basic error resides in making the system of Plotinus synonymous with Neoplatonism; and his suggestion that Plotinus' principle of "participation" enabled the Christian theologians of the Council of Nicea to solve the great problems of the Incarnation and the Trinity is historically inaccurate. [52] Plotinus was an unknown figure to the theologians of Nicea, where, incidentally, the problem of the Incarnation was never discussed. [53] Platonic thought and Neoplatonism were unquestionably instrumental in enabling the theologians of the Councils of Nicea (325 A. D.) and Chalcedon (451 A. D.) to clarify the Christian theology of the Logos. Whether any credit for this clarification can be attributed to Plotinus is impossible to ascertain. [54] Plotinus, in any case, did not present a Christian theologian like Augustine with prefabricated theological formulas. [55] One would have to look hard in Augustine in order to find the formulas of Plotinus in their original form. What Plotinus did give Augustine, however, as the author of the *Confessions* recalls, is a sense of interior exploration, a conviction of the need to return to oneself as a first step toward conversion: "inde admonitus ... intravi in intima mea." [56]

---

[51] *Ibid.*, pp. 1289-93.

[52] *Ibid.*, pp. 1291-92: "C'est en effet selon le principe de participation que le Christianisme va résoudre ses grands problèmes, Incarnation et Trinité...."

[53] A. Vacant, E. Mangenot, E. Amann, *Dictionnaire de Théologie Catholique*, T. XI, 1, art. "Nicée (1.er Concile de)." The major controversy of the Council was the Arian heresy, which taught that the Son (Logos) was created *in time* by the Father, that He was a creature capable of good or evil actions. (See the summary of the Council's decisions, col. 416.) Even if the Council of Nicea had discussed the Incarnation, it is difficult to see how the Plotinian doctrine of participation could have been anything other than a hindrance in resolving the problem.

[54] *Ibid.*, T. II, b, art. "Chalcédoine (Concile de)." Against the Nestorians and the Monophysites, this Council reaffirmed that the Son is consubstantial with the Father; that there are in the Logos two natures, without confusion, transformation, or division; that there is but one person, one hypostasis; that the Son was, in his human nature, born of a Virgin. There is no evidence whatever of a Plotinian "influence" on the language of the dogmatic decrees of Chalcedon.

[55] *Métaphysique Chrétienne...*, in *Essais*, p. 1293.

[56] Augustine, *Confessions*, VII, x, p. 16: "Et inde admonitus redire ad memet ipsum intravi in intima mea." Cf. the same idea in Plotinus, *Enneads*,

So much for the substance of Camus' analysis and the major reservations which they call for. What of his sources? Had he read Plotinus? How did he manage to assimilate the major assertions of such a difficult and arcane system of thought?

His entire chapter on Plotinus is gathered almost exclusively from two sources: Emile Bréhier's *La Philosophie de Plotin,* and René Arnou's *Le Désir de Dieu dans la Philosophie de Plotin.* [57] In this chapter, as elsewhere in his essay on Christian Metaphysics and Neoplatonism, Camus indulges in a favorite practice of copying texts and quotations from secondary sources, while his references indicate that these texts and quotations were gathered from a study of primary sources. The following assertion, for example,

> Il n'y a pas d'être qui ne soit un. Or il n'y a pas d'unité sans forme et sans logos, le logos étant justement le principe d'unité. C'est dire encore qu'il n'y a pas d'être sans âme puisque le logos est l'acte nécessaire de l'âme. [Footnote: *Enneads,* VI, 9, 1] [58]

is not far different from René Arnou:

> Il n'y a pas d'être qui ne soit un. .... Or il n'y a pas d'unité sans forme ou sans logos, le logos étant précisément le principe d'unité.
>
> Donc il n'y a pas d'être sans logos, ou ce qui revient au même, sans âme, car le logos est l'acte nécessaire d'une âme. [59]

This is one of the more glaring illustrations of Camus' method, which consists in reproducing — sometimes verbatim — ideas contained in his secondary sources, while referring the reader to the primary source, as if the discovery were his own.

V, I, i, 23-30: "C'est pourquoi il faut deux raisonnements pour s'adresser à ceux qui sont en cette disposition si l'on veut qu'ils retournent... jusqu'au terme suprême.... L'une montre l'infamie de ce que l'âme honore... la seconde instruit l'âme et lui rappelle en quelque sorte sa race et sa dignité...." Plotin, *Ennéades,* trans. by E. Bréhier (Paris, 1931), pp. 15-16.

[57] E. Bréhier, *La Philosophie de Plotin* (Paris, 1923); R. Arnou, *Le Désir de Dieu dans la Philosophie de Plotin* (Paris, 1921).

[58] A. Camus, *Métaphysique Chrétienne...,* in *Essais,* p. 1272.

[59] R. Arnou, *op. cit.,* p. 87.

Here are a few additional examples:

Camus, *Métaphysique Chrétienne, Essais,* 1965.	E. Bréhier, *La Philosophie de Plotin,* Paris, 1923.
"Mais l'unité d'un ordre est toujours supérieur à cet ordre." (p. 1272.)	"L'unité d'un ordre est donc une réalité supérieure et antérieure à cet ordre lui-même .... " (p. 38.)
"La Réalité métaphysique c'est la vie spirituelle considerée en elle-même." (*Ibid.*)	"La réalité métaphysique est donc la vie spirituelle considerée comme existant en elle-même et par elle-même." (p. 43.)
Camus (*Ibid.*)	R. Arnou, *Le Désir de Dieu,* Paris, 1921.
"Mais le grand problème que la conversion suscite est analogue à celui qu'à trois reprises nous avons trouvé dans la Procession. Il est tout entier posé dans un texte des 'Ennéades': 'Ce qui n'aurait absolument aucune part au Bien, ne saurait désirer le bien.' C'est-à-dire: tu ne me chercherais pas si tu ne m'avais déjà trouvé." (p. 1284.)	" 'Ce qui n'aurait absolument aucune part au Bien ne saurait désirer le Bien .... ' Par voie de conséquence, désirant Dieu du plus profond de son être, l'homme doit déjà posséder Dieu. Tu ne me chercherais pas, si tu ne m'avais déjà trouvé. Cette pensée, que devait immortaliser Pascal, se trouve dans Saint Bernard ... et avant ... dans les Ennéades." (p. 141.)

Camus' analysis of Plotinus, in *Christian Metaphysics,* is essentially a summary of secondary sources. He did, however, consult the original text in Bréhier's translation of the *Enneads,* particularly parts 3, 4. 5 of the fourth *Ennead,* wherein Plotinus discusses "some difficulties concerning the soul." [60] Though it is a hastily composed chapter, and far less impressive than it originally appears once the real sources have been bared, Camus gives a faithful, if sometimes confusing summary of the esoteric system of Plotinus. And his conclusions are not without historical interest and accuracy. The thought of Plotinus, he

---

[60] A. Camus, *Métaphysique Chrétienne,* in *Essais,* pp. 1280-81. Cf. Plotin, *Ennéades,* IV, trans. by E. Bréhier (Paris, 1927), especially pp. 13-22.

says, was quite certainly one of the key factors in Augustine's conversion. And Camus was rightly impressed by some of the incidental aspects of Plotinus' thought: his sensitivity to the beauty of the cosmos, his need to construct a rational mysticism, his use of striking images to express truths too difficult for discursive language. He admired a system wherein the demonstration of truth coincides with a "retour à la chère patrie," [61] wherein the search for transcendence does not turn its back upon the world, wherein the desire for Unity excludes no facet of the multiple universe. To Plotinus, Camus is perhaps indebted for such details as the title of his first collection of essays, and a better understanding of phenomenology. [62] Plotinus was perhaps the only author of Camus' literary experience who managed to reconcile his search for transcendent unity with the conviction that the world of sense is beautiful and irreplaceable. Plotinus taught him that these two aspirations need not be divergent. [63]

A concluding word might be said about the presence of Plotinus in some of Camus' later essays. In "L'Eté à Alger," he writes: "But there are moments when everything [in us] aspires to this homeland of the soul: "Yes, that is the place to which we must return." This union, which Plotinus so ardently wished for, what is so strange about finding it on earth, where unity expresses itself in terms of sun and sea?" [64]

Camus is here alluding to the celebrated φεύγομεν δὴ φίλεις πατρίδα "let us flee to our dear homeland," which he encountered several times in reading Chestov. [65]

In *The Myth of Sisyphus,* he writes:

> It is significant that contemporary thought oscillates ceaselessly between an extreme rationalization of reality, which tends to fragment it into so many "reason-types," and an extreme irrationalization, which tends to deify it.... The

---

[61] *Métaphysique Chrétienne...*, in *Essais*, p. 1271: "cette patrie solitaire du sage...." Cf. Plotinus, *Enneads*, I, 6, 8, pp. 16-24.

[62] *Ibid.*: "Ce n'est pas l'apparence que Plotin recherche mais plutôt *cet envers des choses* qui est son paradis perdu." A collection of essays written by Camus during this same period was entitled *L'Envers et l'Endroit.*

[63] *Ibid.*, pp. 1269-71.

[64] A. Camus, *Noces*, in *Essais*, p. 75.

[65] *Vide* esp. *Les Révélations de la Mort*, trans. by Boris Schloezer (Paris, 1923), pp. 155 and 230.

notion of reason has always, and wrongly, been thought to be a one-way notion. In fact, however rigorous it might be in its ambitions, this concept is no less mobile than others. Reason has a human face, but it can also be turned towards the divine. Plotinus, the first to reconcile reason with the climate of eternity, taught reason to turn away from its dearest principle, that of contradiction, in order to integrate the entirely magical principle of participation. Plotinus effected an adaptation of reason at a time when reason had either to adapt itself or die. [66]

This curious and difficult text can be far better understood in the light of Camus' analysis of the procession of hypostases. The opposition between the divine face of Reason (wherein the Logos is identical with the One), and the human face (wherein the Logos, turned towards the world of appearances, is fragmented into a multiplicity of separate *logoi* or "reason types") is a Plotinian opposition.

Camus' conviction that phenomenology owes much to Plotinus, as well as his assertion that Plotinus "replaced the syllogism with the metaphor" and logic with esthetics, are ideas derived directly from Chestov. [67] In *Christian Metaphysics*, Camus, influenced by Bréhier, underscored the almost rationalistic side of Plotinus' philosophy, whereas in *Noces* and *The Myth,* he stressed the esthetic, intuitive, "illuminationist" side of Plotinus, gathering most of his opinions from Chestov. Might it not be concluded that, between *Christian Metaphysics* (1936) and *The Myth* (1942), Camus identified his comprehesion of Plotinus increasingly with Chestov's?

---

[66] *MS,* in *Essais,* pp. 133-34.
[67] Cf. *Ibid.* and L. Chestov, *Le Pouvoir des Clefs,* pp. 282, and 228-29.

Lucretius' description of the plague of Athens reproduces many of the details of Thucydides' analysis, while it introduces a pathos, a horror, and an apocalyptic grandeur that are lacking in Thucydides' dispassionate diagnosis. [1] That both descriptions served as source material for *The Plague* is demonstrated by an early sketch of the novel, written around 1941, entitled "Exhortation aux Médecins de la Peste." [2] The text is preceded by an epigraph, "Viendra la guerre dorienne et la peste avec elle," to which Camus adds the explanation, "Oracle de Delphes cité par Thucydide." [3] In his description of the Athenian plague, Thucydides does in fact recount that, while the plague was going on, some of the elder Athenians remembered an ambiguous oracle which (as translated from the Greek by Jean Voilquin) reads as follows: "Viendra la guerre dorienne, et avec elle la peste." [4]

The text of the "Exhortation aux Médecins de la Peste" contains several precise references to Thucydides' description of the Athenian plague. Curiously enough, however, while the narrator of the "Exhortation" is purportedly referring to Thucydides, he is in fact copying a French translation of Lucretius:

---

[1] Lucretius, *De Rerum Natura*, VI, vv. 1143 sq.; Thucydides, *The Peloponnesian War*, Book II, chapters XLVII-LIV.

[2] *TRN*, p. 1959, first published in the *Cahiers de la Pleiade*, April, 1947.

[3] "Exhortation aux Médecins de la Peste," in *TRN*, p. 1959.

[4] Thucydide, *Histoire de la Guerre du Péloponnèse*, trans. by J. Voilquin (Paris, 1935), Book II, p. 131. I am assuming, largely on the strength of this textual resemblance, that this was the translation of Thucydides that Camus used. It was also the most up-to-date translation in the early forties.

A. Camus, "Exhortation aux Médecins de la Peste," in *TRN*, Paris, 1965.

Lucrèce, *De la Nature,* trans. by
A. Ernout, vol. II, Paris, 1924.

"Ne donnez pas raison à Thucydide, parlant de la Peste d'Athènes et disant que *les médicins
n'étaient d'aucun secours parce
que dans le principe, ils traitaient
du mal sans le connaître*." (p.
1961.)

"*Les médecins n'étaient d'aucun
secours parce que, dans le principe, ils traitaient du mal sans le
connaître.*" (p. 300, footnote 2:
a translation of *Thuc.,* II, 47, 4.)

"Vous ne cesserez pas d'être cons-
ternés par ces *gorges noires* dont
parle Thucydide, qui *distillent
une* odeur *de sang* et dont *une
toux rauque arrache* avec peine
des *crachats noirs, menus, couleur
de safran et salés . . . .*" (p. 1962.)

"A l'intérieur du corps, la *gorge*
toute *noire distillait une* sueur *de
sang . . .* les *crachats unis, menus,
couleur de safran et salés, arra-
chés avec peine* du gosier par *une
toux rauque.*" (pp. 318 and 320:
a translation of *Lucr.,* VI, vv.
1146-47 and 1187-90.)

"Vous n'entrerez jamais dans la
familiarité de ces *cadavres* dont
même les *oiseaux* de *proie s'écar-
tent pour* en *fuir l'infection.*" (p.
1962.)

"Malgré l'abondance des *cadavres
. . . les oiseaux s'écartaient loin de*
cette *proie pour fuir* l'effroyable
infection." (p. 321; a translation
of *Lucr.,* VI, vv. 1215-18.)

«Et vous continuerez de vous ré-
volter contre cette terrible confusion, où *ceux qui* refusent leurs
soins aux autres *périssent* dans la
solitude tandis que *ceux qui* se
dévouent meurent dans l'entasse-
ment." (p. 1962.)

"Car tous *ceux qui* évitaient soigneusement de visiter leurs parents
malades . . . *périssaient* abandon-
nés . . . . *Ceux* au contraire *qui*
n'avaient point quitté les *leurs
. . .* succombaient, eux aussi, à la
contagion . . ." (p. 322; a translation of *Lucr.,* VI, vv. 1238-44.)

One of the characters that Camus had intended to portray in
his early version of *The Plague,* it will be remembered, was a young
professor of classical literature named Stéphan. The plague was to
teach this young man "that he had never until now understood Thu-
cydies and Lucretius." [5] Quite significantly, Stéphan disappears from
the final version of the novel, as do most of the direct references to

---

[5] *Carnets,* I, p. 230.

Lucretius and Thucydides. There does remain at least one conscious imitation of the closing description of the *De Rerum Natura*:

A. Camus, *La Peste*, in *TRN*, Paris, 1965.	Lucretius, *De Rerum Natura*, trans. by A. Ernout, Paris, 1964.
"Et le docteur Rieux, qui regardait le golfe, pensait à ces bûchers dont parle Lucrèce et que les Athéniens frappés par la maladie élevaient devant la mer. On y portait les morts durant la nuit, mais la place manquait et les vivants se battaient à coups de torches pour y placer ceux qui leur avaient été chers, *soutenant des luttes sanglantes plutôt que d'abandonner leurs cadavres.* (pp. 1247-48.)	«Mainte horreur s'accomplit, que la nécessité de l'heure et la pauvreté conseillèrent. Et l'on en vit qui, sur des bûchers dressés pour d'autres, plaçaient à grands cris les corps de leurs proches, et en approchaient la torche enflammée, *soutenant des luttes sanglantes plutôt que d'abandonner leurs cadavres.* (VI, 1280-86.)

Thucydides' presence in the final version of *The Plague* is decidedly less explicit than in the earlier fragment. Though his name is not once mentioned, several passages of the novel bear what strikes this reader as the unmistakable Thucydidean imprint; and so well does the substance of the Greek text seem to have been assimilated that it seems hardly an exaggeration to speak of a conscious imitation.

Like his classical model, the narrator of the events of Oran claims to have eschewed all forms of literary artifice. Camus' narrator wishes to avoid "modifying anything with artistic effects, save those which answer the needs of an approximately coherent account." [6] Thucydides, too, prefers to sacrifice literary charm for the sake of sobriety and clarity and warns his reader that, though "it may well by that my history will seem less easy to read because of the absence in it of a romantic element ... it will be enough for me ... if these words of mine are judged useful by those who want to understand clearly the events which happened in the past...." [7]

Camus' narrator, like Thucydides, deems it necessary to inform his reader about the nature of his documents and sources. Rieux enu-

---

[6] *La Peste*, in *TRN*, p. 1363.
[7] Thucydides, *The Peloponnesian War*, trans. by Rex Warner (Penguin Books, 1956), p. 24.

merates three types of documents: his own testimony, the confidential information provided him by the personae of his chronicle, and the texts which happened to fall into his hands. [8] Thucydides assures his reader that "with regard to my factual reporting of the events of the war... either I was present myself at the events which I have described or else I heard of them from eye-witnesses whose reports I have checked with as much thoroughness as possible." [9]

Both narrators employ similar phraseology in describing the super-human dimensions of the plague. "Le fléau *n'était pas à la mesure de l'homme*...." declares Camus' narrator. [10] Thucydides calls it "beyond the capacity of human nature to endure." [11] Even the symptoms of the plague of Oran seem to a large extent "borrowed" from Thucydides. A comparison of Camus' description of the plague symptoms with the translation of Thucydides he quite probably used reveals a number of verbal and syntactical similarities:

A. Camus, *La Peste, in TRN,* Paris, 1965.	Thucydide, *Histoire de la guerre du Peloponnèse,* trans. by J. Voilquin, vol. I (Paris, 1935), book II, chapters 48-49.
"Il fallait s'en tenir à ce qu'on savait, la stupeur et la prostration, *les yeux rouges, la bouche sale, les maux de tête,* les bubons, *la soif terrible,* le délire, *les taches sur le corps, l'écartèlement intérieur*.... (pp. 1246-47.)	"...je me contenterai d'en décrire les caractères et les symptômes capables de faire diagnostiquer le mal.... On éprouvait de violentes chaleurs *à la tête; les yeux étaient rouges* et enflammés, le pharynx et la langue devenaient sanguinolents, la respiration irrégulière, l'haleine fétide.... La peau ... était rougeâtre ... mais *à l'intérieur* le corps était en proie *à une soif inextinguible* ... La plupart mouraient .... consumés par *le feu intérieur*." (pp. 127-28.)

---

[8] *La Peste,* in *TRN,* pp. 1219-20: "son témoignage d'abord, celui des autres ensuite... et, en dernier lieu, les textes qui finirent par tomber entre ses mains."

[9] *The Peloponnesian War,* trans. by Warner, p. 24.

[10] *La Peste,* in *TRN,* p. 1245.

[11] *The Peloponnesian War,* trans. by R. Warner, p. 125.

As a result of the plague, the citizens of Oran, like the Athenians, are "cut off from the outer world," exiled. In both cases a barrier separates the inner from the outer world. While the Athenians die within their walls, their outside territory is being laid waste by the enemy. [12] Camus' narrator stresses both the physical and the moral barriers inside which, under the pressure of misery, the citizens of Oran stubbornly immure themselves:

> In the general exile they [the outsiders who were trapped in Oran] were the most exiled.... they were obsessed by it [i.e. space] and at every moment knocked their heads against the walls of this huge and alien lazar-house secluding them from their lost homes. ... As for that outside world, which can always offer an escape from everything, they [the outsiders] shut their eyes to it, bent as they were on cherishing the all-too-real phantoms of their imagination.... [13]

The plague-ridden inhabitants of both cities attempt to find solace in memories, signs, and omens. The citizens of Oran "fed their despondency with fleeting intimations, messages as disconcerting as a flight of swallows." [14] As for the Athenians, they began to recall old oracles; and such was their confusion towards past and present that "it was a case of people adapting their memories to suit their sufferings." [15]

In Oran, as in Athens, all wordly ambitions and traditional drives are reduced to nothing. The citizens of Oran "no longer made any choice. The plague had suppressed all value judgments. They accepted everything en bloc." [16] As for the Athenians, to whom "money and life alike seemed equally ephemeral," they were "generally agreed that what was both honorable and valuable was the pleasure of the moment and everything that might conceivably contribute to that pleasure." [17] As to religion, Camus' narrator describes an "objective"

---

[12] *Ibid.*, p. 127. For the Greek text I have consulted Thucydide, *La Guerre du Péloponnèse*, ed. and trans. by J. de Romilly (Paris, 1962), Book II, ch. 50, p. 129.

[13] A. Camus, *The Plague*, trans. by S. Gilbert (New York, 1947), p. 67.

[14] *Ibid.*

[15] *The Peloponnesian War*, trans. by R. Warner, p. 127.

[16] A. Camus, *La Peste*, in *TRN*, p. 1366.

[17] *The Peloponnesian War*, trans. by R. Warner, p. 127.

state of mind, while Thucydides underscores the indiscriminateness of human destiny towards the Athenians:

A. Camus, *La Peste*, in *TRN*, Paris, 1965.	Thucydides, *The Peloponnesian War*, trans. by Rex Warner (Penguin Books, 1956, Book II.)
"With regard to religion, as to many other problems, the plague had put them in a singular frame of mind, as far removed from passion as from indifference, which one could quite accurately describe with the word 'objectivity'." (p. 1293.)	"No fear of god or law of man had a restraining influence. As for the gods, it seemed to be the same thing whether one worshipped them or not, when one saw the good and the bad dying indiscriminately." (p. 127.)

Both the Athenians and the citizens of Oran bury their dead with a singular dispatch. Camus' narrator is particularly sensitive to the effects of these quick burials on "natural feelings," morale, and dignity. Thucydides, ever the objective observer, measures the adverse consequences of these burials on religion, law, and custom:

A. Camus, *The Plague*, trans. by S. Gilbert, N. Y., 1947.	Thucydides, *The Peloponnesian War*, trans. by Rex Warner (Penguin Books, 1954), Book II.
"The whole process was put through with the maximum of speed and the minimum of risk. It cannot be denied that, anyhow in the early days, the *natural feelings* of the family were somewhat outraged by these lightning funerals. But obviously in time of plague such *sentiments* can't be taken into account, and all was sacrificed to efficiency. And though, to start with, the *morale* of the population was shaken by this summary procedure — for the desire to have a "proper" funeral is more widespread than is generally believed — as time went on ... the	"For the catastrophe was so overwhelming that men, not knowing what would happen next to them, became indifferent to every rule of *religion* or *law*. All the funeral *ceremonies* which used to be observed were now disorganized, and they buried the dead as best they could. Many people ... adopted the most shameless methods. They would arrive first at a funeral that had been made by others, put their own dead upon it and set it alight; or, finding another pyre burning, they would throw the corpse that they were carrying on top of the other one and go away." (p. 126.)

thoughts of our townsfolk were
diverted to more instant needs."
(p. 158.)

* * *

Thus far I have dealt with Camus' use of Lucretius and Thucydides in the genesis of one of his major works, *The Plague*. [18] So far
as one can tell, there are few other evocations of Thucydides in
Camus' work, with the notable exception of the speech given by "La
Peste," in *The State of Siege*, wherein Camus is once again referring
to a French translation of *The Peloponnesian War*. [19]

Lucretius is another matter. In a sense, it is only by an extension
of the meaning of the term Hellenism that one is justified in including
the great Latin poet among Camus' "Hellenic" sources. It is an extension, however, that Camus would not only have approved, but
indeed considered necessary. Though Camus never disguised what it
is not excessive to call his "hostility" towards the Latin spirit, he
did not consider Lucretius as Latin, but as Greek. [20] One need
not recall Camus' admiration of Lucretius' "fearful melancholy"
in the presence of the cosmic cycles — he quoted the "sunt eadem
omnia semper" as early as *Christian Metaphysics*—, and his tragic

---

[18] I am not the first to have attempted a *rapprochement* between Thucydides and Camus. In *La Mer et les Prisons*, Roger Quilliot, the distinguished
editor of both "Pleiade" volumes of Camus' works, took notice of the "inci-
sive reflections *à la manière de Thucydide*" that cap each chapter of *The
Plague*. I have attempted to show that some of the concision, the irony,
the lucidity, even the language of *The Plague* are written "à la manière de
Thucydide."

[19] The tirade by "*La Peste*," in *L'Etat de Siège*, contains literal echoes
of Thucydides: "La Peste" declares: "Mes morts ont fécondé les sables de la
Lybie et de la noire Ethiopie. . . . J'ai rempli Athènes des feux de la purification, allumé sur ses plages des milliers de bûchers funèbres, couvert la
mer grecque de cendres humaines jusqu'à la rendre grise . . . ." (A. Camus,
Théâtre, Récits, Nouvelles [Paris, 1962], p. 295. All subsequent references
to this volume will be indicated as *TRN*.) Cf. Thucydides, *La Guerre du
Péloponnèse*, trans. by J. de Romilly, Book II, ch. XLIII: "[La peste] fit,
dit-on, sa première apparition en Ethiopie . . . puis elle descendit en Egypte,
en Lybie et dans la plupart des territoires du grand roi. Athènes se vit frap-
per brusquement. . . . "

[20] For Camus' hostility towards things Roman, see especially his "Poli-
tique et Culture Méditerranéenne," in *Essais*, pp. 1324 and *passim*: "Ce
n'est pas la vie que Rome a prise à la Grèce, mais l'abstraction puérile et
raisonnante."

courage in facing the certainty of his own dissolution. [21] In *The Rebel,* Lucretius' system is summarized along with that of Epicurus as though it were but an accident of literary history (which indeed it was) that Lucretius had written in Latin and not in Greek.

Anyone who has had the pleasure of reading Simone Fraisse's article on "the contradictions of revolt" in Lucretius and Camus can only deem it pretentious to desire to contribute anything further to a comparative study of their systems. [22] Since the purpose of Simone Fraisse's article, however, was to confront the responses of both Camus and Lucretius to similar metaphysical problems, rather than deal with the latter's literary influence on the former, it might be pertinent to deal with Lucretius' poem as a sourcebook for *The Rebel,* as previously I have done for *The Plague.*

When he discusses the problem of metaphysical rebellion in Lucretius, Camus sets a number of texts in quotation marks. The reader of "The Sons of Cain" understandably assumes that Camus has set these texts of Lucretius in quotation marks because they are a reminiscence, a paraphrase, or, at best, a quotation from memory, of some unspecified verses from the *De Rerum Natura.* Only after a painstaking foray into Alfred Ernout's translation of Lucretius' poem does the Camus scholar discover that Camus is quoting specific Lucretian verses, and from a specific edition:

A. Camus, *L'Homme Révolté,* in *Essais,* Paris, 1965.	Lucrèce, *De Rerum Natura,* trans. by A. Ernout, Paris, 1964.
"La substance de ce vaste monde est réservée à la mort et à la ruine." (p. 440.)	"Et l'on n'ose pas croire que la substance de ce vaste monde est réservée à la mort et à la ruine." (VI, 565-66.)
"Il est incontestable que les dieux, par *leur* nature même, jouissent de l'immortalité au milieu de la paix la plus profonde, étrangers à nos affaires dont ils sont tout à fait détachés." (p. 44.)	"Car il est incontestable que les dieux, par *la* nature même, jouissent de l'immortalité au milieu de la paix la plus profonde, étrangers à nos affaires, dont ils sont tout à fait détachés." (II, 646-48.)

[21] *Métaphysique Chrétienne . . . ,* ni *Essais,* p. 1228. Cf. *L'Homme Révolté,* in *Essais,* pp. 442-43.

[22] S. Fraisse, "Lucrèce et Camus," *Esprit,* March, 1959.

"*Mœnia mundi,* les remparts du monde." (p. 442.)

"les remparts du monde." (I, 1102.)

"La piété, pour Lucrèce, est sans doute de pouvoir tout regarder d'un esprit que rien ne trouble." (p. 442.)

"La piété, ce n'est point se montrer à tout instant, couvert d'un voile ... mais c'est plutôt pouvoir tout regarder d'un esprit que rien ne trouble." (V, 1198-1203.)

«On y parle de ce trait divin qui souvent passe à côté des coupables et va, par un châtiment immérité, priver de la vie des innocents." (p. 443.)

«Qui donc pourrait ... lancer ce trait qui souvent passe à côté des coupables et va, par un châtiment immerité, priver de la vie des innocents?" (II, 1097-1104.)

"Epicure lui-même, dans l'épopée de Lucrèce, deviendra le rebelle magnifique qu'il n'était pas. Alors qu'aux yeux de tous, l'humanité traînait sur terre une vie abjecte, écrasée sous le poids d'une religion *dont le visage se montrait* du haut des régions célestes, *menaçant* les mortels de son aspect horrible, le premier, un Grec, un homme, osa lever ses yeux mortels contre elle, et contre elle se dresser .... Et, par là, la religion est à son tour renversée et foulée aux pieds, et nous, la victoire nous élève jusqu'aux cieux." (p. 443.)

"Alors qu'aux yeux de tous, l'humanité traînait sur terre une vie abjecte, ecrasée sous le poids d'une religion *dont le visage, se montrant* du haut des régions célestes, *menaçait* les mortels de son aspect horrible, le premier, un Grec, un homme, osa lever ses yeux mortels contre elle, et contre elle se dresser .... Et par là, la religion est à son tour renversée et foulée aux pieds, et nous, la victoire nous élève jusqu'aux cieux." (I, 61-79.)

It is fair to conclude that Camus' master and guide through the labyrinth of the Lucretian poem was Alfred Ernout's translation, which stands on its own as a remarkable piece of French prose. From the "suave mari magno ..." to the Wagneresque funeral pyres at the end of Book VI, Ernout's translation manages to convey the tragic serenity, the incomparable sense of urgency, that still today make of Lucretius the most readable of Latin poets. It is not surprising that, while he scribbled out the first drafts of what was to become *The Plague,* Camus should have incorporated Ernout's Lucretius into the fabric of his very text; and it is still less surprising that, nearly a decade later, while writing *The Rebel,* he could pay Ernout's text the same silent tribute.

CHAPTER II

THE EXILE OF HELEN: HELLENISM AND CHRISTIANITY

Had he never read a single line of Nietzsche, Camus would still surely have contracted the habit of opposing Hellenism to Christianity. To begin with, the influence of Greek ideas on Christianity had always been one of his favorite topics of interest. [1] He had, moreover, an innate gift or compulsion for reflecting in antithetical terms, particularly with regard to this historical problem. "A burdensome heritage it is," he wrote, "to be born in a pagan land in Christian times ... I feel closer to the values of the ancient world than to Christian values." [2] Greece he considered as the "very negation" of Rome and of the Latin "spirit of abstraction," which Catholic Christianity had incorporated into its very fabric. "Give us the Doric Apollos," he exclaimed in an early lecture on the "Mediterranean spirit," "not the Vatican imitations!" [3]

Camus' habit of considering Hellenism and Christianity in resolutely antithetical terms was more than the product of a mere instinctive disposition. His earliest readings on Hellenism had made the antithesis seem like a historical necessity. Nietzsche's relentless attacks against "two thousand years of antinature" had, of course, played the leading role in endowing Camus with this particular optic. [4]

---

[1] Cf. Jean Grenier, *Albert Camus* (Paris, 1968), p. 42.

[2] Interview recorded in *Les Nouvelles Littéraires*, May 10, 1951, reprinted in *Essais*, p. 1343.

[3] "Inaugural Lecture at the 'Maison de la Culture' (Algiers)," February 8, 1937, quoted in *Essais*, p. 1324.

[4] F. Nietzsche, *Extrait d'Ecce Homo*, in *La Naissance de la Tragédie*, trans. by G. Bianquis (Paris, 1949), pp. 145-46. As in chapted one, I shall refer to the French translations of Nietzsche used by Camus himself.

But Nietzsche had not been alone. Louis Rougier, whose book on Celsus left its mark on *Christian Metaphysics and Neoplatonism,* had described Hellenism as an essentially polemical weapon that had developed out of the final struggle between the new religion and the old pagan philosophy. [5] In Christian apologetic literature from the middle of the second century onwards, argued Rougier, "Hellene" is synonymous with "Pagan." For the first generation of Christian apologists, a Greek was simply anyone that refused to accept the religion of the Nazarene. In a discourse to "the Greeks," written around the year 170 A. D., Tatian had chided the cultured despisers of Christianity for their stiff-neckedness; and, in the third century, Origen had made no attempt to disguise his hostily towards a still vital secular philosophy, which he referred to as "Hellenic demonstration." Pagan writers, on the other hand, rallied round the word "Hellenism" like soldiers round a flag preparing for the enemy's final charge. At the end of the fourth century, Macarius Magnus dubbed Porphyry, that eloquent and uncompromising Neoplatonist, as "the defender of Hellenic glory." [6] The Emperor Julian, the most ardent protagonist of the "Pagan reaction," stands as the first Greek writer to have used the substantive *hellenismós* in order to designate the rites of a somewhat floundering Greek religion, as opposed to those of the "Jewish" religion. In a letter to Arsacius, the High-Priest of Galicia, Julian described *hellenismós* as the system of religious and ethical values into which he was attempting to breathe new life, in order to shore them up against the tide of Christianity. Those remaining faithful to these ancient values Julian called *Hellenistás,* or *Hellenikoús.* Christianity, on the other hand, he dismisses as "atheism." [7]

Had he used the word "Hellenism" exclusively as a polemical term, therefore, Camus would have been following a literary tradition that is nearly as old as Christianity. It would have been uncharacteristic of Camus, however, to use the term in such an exclusive, almost vindictive sense. Surely, thought Camus, Hellenism was far more than a term of exclusion; and surely it was unfair to pretend that the Greek and Christian universes were unalterably opposed. "It is always

---

[5] Louis Rougier, *Celse* (Paris, 1926), p. 61.

[6] *Ibid.,* pp. 61-66.

[7] L'Empereur Julien, *Œuvres Complètes,* Vol. I, trans. by J. Bridez (Paris, 1924), pp. 144-46.

arbitrary," he argues in *Christian Metaphysics,* to speak of a 'Greek spirit' as opposed to a 'Christian spirit.' Aeschylus and Sophocles, the primitive masks and the Panathenaïc games . . . , the religious mysteries and Socrates — everything points to the presence alongside the 'Greece of light' of a 'Greece of darkness,' less classical but equally real." [8]

While he was aware of Nietzsche's contempt for "Socratic serenity," Camus never allowed Nietzsche to spoil his appreciation of what he considered one of the most characteristic Hellenic traits, Greek rationalism. He does not hesitate to praise the Greeks' metaphysical and moral intellectualism, their conviction that the universe "can be entirely understood," that "virtue is something that can be learned." [9] He admires the Greeks' sense of harmony, their "athletic and esthetic justification of existence," their universe "centered entirely about man and his effort." [10] Camus' vision of Greece, in the final analysis, is far more classical and comprehensive than that of Nietzsche, who seems to have reserved his finest ironies for those elements that Camus valued most — reason, equilibrium, moral optimism. [11] How remote does an "athletic and esthetic justification of existence" seem from Nietzsche's idea of a primitive Greece that sublimates its suffering in Dionysian song!

Camus' general conception of the Greek universe was laden with the ambiguities, the contradictions, and the confusions that were those of Greek civilization itself. Any term such as "Hellenism," or "Greek universe," when it is meant to embody nearly ten centuries of civilization, is exposed to the peril of ambiguity. No body of literature that includes both Homer's description of Achilles' buckler and Plotinus' vision of the First Hypostasis can possibly be summarized in a meaningful term. Camus realized what historical risks were involved in talking about "Hellenism," "Greece," or "the "Greek universe." Yet, though he would have been the first to concede that the Greece of the *kouroi* was not the Greece of Menander, and that both might

---

[8] *Métaphysique Chrétienne,* in *Essais,* p. 1309.

[9] *Ibid.,* p. 1226.

[10] *Ibid.*

[11] Cf., for example, the opening pages of *Christian Metaphysics* (*Essais,* pp. 1224-48) with Nietzsche's evaluation of the alleged "golden equilibrium" of the Greeks ("Le Crépuscule des faux dieux," in *La Naissance de la Tragédie,* trans. by G. Bianquis, pp. 138-39).

have appeared identical next to the Greece of the Hellenistic age, he knew that the need remained for an operative general term. "It is quite certain," he remarks in *Christian Metaphysics,* "that one can extract from a civilization a certain number of favorite themes and 'privileged designs' which, when considered together, comprise what is commonly called Hellenism." [12] In order to know which elements of Greek thought prefigured Christianity, and which rejected the new religion in advance, Camus realized that a historical study of their confrontation was a necessity. *Christian Metaphysics and Neoplatonism* was the young Camus' account of the confrontation. "I had always been interested in this problem," he later confided to Jean Grenier, "and it is not a coincidence that I chose it as the subject of my *diplôme.*"

* * *

How had Hellenism and Christianity, with their supposedly opposite visions of the universe, ever managed to fuse into one another? Such was the historical problem that Camus had attempted to resolve. The progressive Hellenization of Christianity, he argued, had traversed four distinct phases. First, there had appeared the Christianity of the Gospels, as yet uninfluenced by Greek philosophy. Then, in an initial encounter between Greek rationalism and Christian revelation, there had occurred the Gnostics' attempt to Hellenize Christian mysteries; but this attempt had led to the most exaggerated conclusions. In a third phase, Neoplatonism had provided the Christian theologians, particularly Augustine, with the intellectual formulas they needed to convert the message of the Gospels into a philosophy. The fourth and final step had been the Augustinian "second revelation," which achieved the transformation of Christian revelation into a metaphysics, and allowed Christianity to conquer its universality. [13]

What philosophical and religious climate had favored the encounter of Christian and Greek ideas? What changes had the Hellenic sensibility previously undergone, that it should merge so painlessly

---

[12] *Métaphysique Chrétienne . . .,* in *Essais,* p. 1225.

[13] *Ibid.,* p. 1230. Each of these "phases" corresponds to one of the four chapters of *Christian Metaphysics,* in *Essais,* pp. 1236-1310: "Evangelical Christianity," pp. 1231-1250; "Gnosis," pp. 1250-1269; "Mystical Reason," pp. 1269-1293; "The Second Revelation," pp. 1293-1310.

with the new religion? To his own query Camus retorts that the "fusion" of Hellenism and Christianity was neither as painless nor as foreordained as appears in retrospect. Even around the time of Christ, many of the old Greek notions would have seemed to reject Christianity in advance. The ancient Greek idea that life is essentially an esthetic phenomenon, that man is the measure of all things, that morality is a matter of knowledge and immorality a matter of ignorance, that Nature includes the entire spectrum of being, that the world is eternal and cyclical — such attitudes could not be reconciled with the Christian notions of sin, grace, redemption, creation *ex nihilo*, and bodily resurrection after death. [14]

In other respects the Hellenistic world provided an incomparably fertile soil for Christianity to grow and spread. The desire for God, during the tormented centuries that followed the Alexandrian conquests, became a more important life-goal than simply "living the beautiful life." The continued popularity of the Eleusinian mysteries indicated that many continued to feel the need for purification and initiation to the underworld. [15] Never had the Oriental religions been so popular, widespread, or variegated. The Mediterranean heaven (as Camus describes it) was inhabited by a motley assortment of divinities: Gnostic eons, the Judaic Yahweh, the Christian Father, the Plotinian hypostases, even remnants of the old Roman divinities, still being worshipped in the Italian countryside. [16] The search for God, an Oriental adventure, was beginning to replace the Greek search for the Good. Pride in life was being substituted by spiritual humility. "The painful drama of Isis in search of Osiris is being enacted. One dies with Dionysus and rises again with him. Attis is being subjected to the worst mutilations. At Eleusis, Zeus is being united with Demeter.... The desire for God, humility, the need for regeneration — themes such as these appear in the mysteries and the Oriental religions of Mediterranean paganism. From the second century B. C. onwards, the main religions of the Mediterranean basin are preparing the way for Christianity." [17]

---

[14] *Métaphysique Chrétienne...*, in *Essais*, pp. 1225-26.

[15] *Ibid.*, p. 1226.

[16] *Ibid.*, p. 1227.

[17] *Ibid.*, p. 1228. Camus' description of the religious situation in the Mediterranean during that period in question is generally accurate. Cf. a

If Christianity was prefigured in the aspirations common to the various religious and philosophical systems that preceded it, the gospels still had a distinctive character of their own. The Incarnation represented, in Camus' own words, "the privileged theme ... , the natural solution to the aspirations of the period." [18] The "extraordinary adventure" of a God's assuming the sins, humiliations, and miseries of mankind, an idea both strange and repulsive to the Hellenic mind, explains why the earliest Christian communities were filled at the same time with pessimism and hope. [19] The universe, on the one hand, was supposed to end at any moment. The founder of the Christian religion had himself undergone an ignominious death. The central religious experience of death, coupled with the certitude that the *parousia* was imminent, filled the Christians with contempt for the world. An overriding sense of sin confirmed them in their conviction that the human condition was an unremitting struggle against evil. [20]

Such was the dark side of the Christian message; but the Incarnation had once for all provided the key to this mystery. The Kingdom of God was henceforth to be at the center of man's preoccupations, and preparing it meant renouncing everything else. Since Time, moreover, was the stage on which the drama of that Kingdom was being enacted, history began to be considered, not as an endless repetition of cycles, but as the hidden design of God. [21] The perennial problems of Greek philosophy could now be stated in terms of time, space, and matter. It was not the immortality of the soul that preoccupied the Christian, as it had Plato, but whether on the last day his risen body would be among the elect or the damned. The Heracleitean theme of the eternal return receded in favor of a divine interpretation of history, a dynamic universe created and redeemed by God, and awaiting its eventual annihilation. Belief was considered superior to understanding. The faith of fools, as Saint Paul had told the Corinthians, had put the wisdom of the philosophers to shame. Well into the second

---

similar description by the noted Hellenist A. Festugière, *L'Enfant d'Agrigente* (Paris, 1950), p. 117.

[18] *Ibid.*, p. 1231.

[19] *Ibid.*, p. 1232.

[20] *Ibid.*, p. 1234.

[21] *Ibid.*, p. 1236: "La philosophie de l'histoire, notion étrangère à un esprit grec, est une invention judaïque."

century of the new era, Christian literature remained contemptuous of all philosophical speculation. "Is there anything common," asked Tertullian, "between Athens and Jerusalem, between the Academy and the Church? . . . For ourselves, we have no curiosity outside of Jesus Christ, no research outside the gospels." [22] Like Tertullian in the Latin Church, Greek writers of the second and third centuries like Saints Clement, Ignatius and Polycarp devoted their attention to the religious dimension of every problem, to the exclusion of every other. [23]

As more and more educated Greeks began to convert to the new religion, however, Christianity had to adopt a more mellow and utilitarian view of Hellenic philosophy. Towards the end of the second century, Justin was already hinting at the resemblances between Christian doctrine and some Greek philosophical tenets. And Clement of Alexandria began to chide the Christian "know-nothings" of his day for their simple-minded fear of Greek philosophy: "The crowd is as fearful of Greek philosophy as children are of a scarecrow . . . . " [24] Clement's admonitions, like those of other Christian writers with little or no inclination for cutting themselves off from the rich tradition in which their intellects had been nourished, were gradually successful in persuading the "simpliciores" that they really had nothing to fear. And so Greek philosophy was slowly but surely readmitted, not as a primary vehicle of truth, but, in Clement's words, "as a product of human intelligence." [25]

It was this combination of evangelical faith and Greek metaphysics, Camus argues, that produced the Christian dogmas. That fusion, needless to relate, did not take place in a day. Many contradictions had to be overcome, and not a few obstacles either overcome or skirted. The Christian belief in an *ex nihilo* creation could not easily nor soon be reconciled with Aristotle's cycles, or even with Plato's demiurge. (How could a perfect God create an imperfect substance if, as Christianity pretended, there were no intermediaries between the conception and the execution?) Rather than spend its time reconsidering classical problems of the mind such as this, Christianity set about giving an intellectual formulation to a series of themes which

---

[22] *Ibid.,* p. 1244.
[23] *Ibid.,* pp. 1239-43.
[24] *Ibid.,* pp. 1243-44.
[25] *Ibid.,* p. 1244.

had originally been meant to appeal to the heart rather than the
intellect. Evangelical Christianity had found itself out of joint with
the times; Greek thought enabled it to reconcile itself with the philosophical world, in short, to ask for its intellectual visa. Such was the
task reserved for the most eminent doctors of the early Church —
Clement, Origin, and especially Saint Augustine. [26]

The Hellenization of Christianity was neither a smooth nor a
homogeneous process. Gnosticism, with its plethora of eons and intermediaries, its radical separation of the universe into two antagonis-
tic camps, "showed Christianity the road it should not take." [27] Span-
ning more than two centuries, Gnosticism was an agglomeration of
the rampant religious confusions of the second and third centuries;
it was (in Camus' own terms) "a monstrous Christianity, a composite
of Oriental religion and Greek mythology." [28] They were "obsessed
with the problem of evil , . . . pessimistic in their outlook towards the
world. They prayed God with the greatest possible fervor, yet considered Him unattainable. From their emotional conception of the
divinity, Christianity derived the idea of God's omnipotence and of
man's nothingness. Gnosticism considered knowledge as a means
of salvation. In this regard it was Greek, for it was convinced that
illumination of the mind necessarily entails a regeneration of the soul.
Gnosticism, in a sense, elaborated a Greek theory of Grace." [29]

With the assistance of Neoplatonism, Augustine managed to resolve the two intellectual problems that had kept him from embracing
Christianity: the nature of evil, and the relation of the Logos to the
Father. It was Plotinus, especially, that provided the greatest and
the most philosophical of the Christian Fathers with the "ready-made
formulas" he needed to phrase the major dogmas of the Christian
religion and to defend them against heresy. With Augustine, the Hellenization of Christianity was complete. His work marks the end of
the primitive age of Christianity and the beginning of its universality. The most important moment of its evolution had been its break
with Judaism and its entrance into the Hellenistic world. The collision

---

[26] *Ibid.*, p. 1249.
[27] *Ibid.*
[28] *Ibid.*, p. 1268.
[29] *Ibid.*

of Mediterranean thought with the gospel revelation produced a reaction, for which Neoplatonism had provided the catalyst. [30]

* * *

The characteristic failure of *Christian Metaphysics,* as I have several times indicated elsewhere, is that Camus' information was badly digested. [31] While it would be unfair to accuse him of outright plagiarism (except, perhaps, for some passages in chapters three and four), he does regularly borrow nearly the totality of his material from secondary sources, while his footnote references are meant to give the impression that his work is either his own, or the result of exhaustive inquiry into primary sources. The general introduction and the first chapter of the essay are a case in point. While Camus' debt to scholars such as Louis Rougier, Franz Cumont, Emile Bréhier, Alfred Loisy, and J. Tixeront is staggering, he credits them with but a fraction of what they in fact provided him. Thus, for example, one reads in the introduction that, "En un certain sens les Grecs acceptaient *une justification sportive et esthétique de l'existence....* Leur évangile disait: notre Royaume est de ce monde. C'est le 'Tout ce qui t'accomode, Cosmos, m'accomode,' de Marc Aurèle." [32]

To sustain this resonant assertion, Camus gives a precise reference to Marcus Aurelius' *Pensées,* IV, 23.

In his study of Celsus, Louis Rougier (who was even fonder than Camus of historical generalizations), declares that "L'Hellène s'accomodait volontiers *d'une justification sportive et esthétique de l'existence,*" and quotes the identical text from Marcus Aurelius. [33] It is reasonable to suspect that, in this instance at least, Camus did not take the trouble of consulting Marcus Aurelius, or even of verifying Rougier's reference. Thus does Camus regularly proceed, throughout *Christian Metaphysics;* and if his reader is fortunate or wily enough to locate the unacknowledged sources that underlie each chapter, he can almost piece the chapter together like a jig-saw puzzle. Thus, for example, Camus' comparison of the historical differences between

---

[30] *Ibid.,* p. 1306.

[31] Cf., in particular, my criticism of Camus' use of sources in chapter four.

[32] *Métaphysique Chrétienne,* in *Essais,* p. 1225.

[33] Louis Rovgier, *op. cit.,* "Preface," p. xxix.

Hellenism and Christianity, in the general introduction, is a patchwork of texts and phrases borrowed from Rougier's book, without acknowledgment: [34]

A. Camus, *Métaphysique Chrétienne*, in *Essais*, Paris, 1965.

L. Rougier, *Celse*, Paris, 1965.

" . . . les Grecs ne pouvaient comprendre *le dogme d'une résurrection charnelle. Celse, Porphyre, et Julien* par exemple *n'ont pas assez de railleries à cet égard.*"
(p. 1226.)

"Contre *l'idée de la résurrection des corps, Celse, Porphyre, Julien* ne tarissent pas de sarcasmes."
(p. 86.)

"Cette *conception purement rationnelle de la vie* . . . *conduit à l'intellectualisme moral*: la vertu est chose qui s'apprend . . . . Si donc le mal moral est une ignorance ou une erreur, comment insérer dans cette attitude les notions de *Rédemption* et de *Péché?*"
(p. 1226.)

"Ce qui caractérise la pensée grecque, c'est son effort pour parvenir à une *conception purement rationelle* de l'Univers et *de la vie*. Ce rationnalisme *conduit à l'intellectualisme en morale*, qui exclut la doctrine paulinienne du *péché*, de la *rédemption* et de la grâce."
(p. 67.)

The second section of his general introduction, which describes the "common religious aspirations" of the Mediterranean world during the Hellenistic age, is essentially a *réchauffé* of Franz Cumont's and Alfred Loisy's studies of Oriental and pagan mysteries. [35] The inaccuracy of some of Camus' references provide some idea of the haste with which he must have written this section, not to say the entire essay. In describing the religious climate that was generated by the pagan mysteries of the centuries immediately preceding the time of Christ, Camus asserts that "the Greek sense of esthetic contemplation was superseded by a tragic sense of life, which concentrated man's aspirations on an imitation of God." [36] He then sustains this view with a bizarre reference to Alfred Loisy's *Mystères Paiens*: "La

---

[34] From the opening section of *Métaphysique Chrétienne* . . ., in *Essais*, pp. 1224-26.

[35] *Ibid.*, pp. 1226-30. Cf. Franz Cumont, *Les Religions Orientales dans le Paganisme Romain* (Paris, 1907), p. 5 and passim; Alfred Loisy, *Les Mystères Paiens et le Mystère Chrétien*, Paris, 1919.

[36] *Ibid.*, p. 1227.

déesse Brimo a enfanté Brimos." *Philosoph.*: V, 8. Cf. Plutarque, de Iside, 27 apud Loisy: *Mystères paiens et mystère chrétien*, ch. IV, p. 139. "Après avoir comprimé et étouffé la rage de Typhon [Isis] ne voulut pas que les combats qu'elle avait soutenus tombassent dans l'oubli et le silence. *Elle institua donc des initiations très simples où seraient représentées par des images, des allégories et par des scènes figurées les souffrances de sa lutte.*" [37]

The mysterious first sentence, one discovers, is to be found somewhere in Loisy's book. [38] It is quoted completely out of context, and it fails to demonstrate anything whatsoever about a "tragic sense of life," or an "imitation of God." As for the rest of the quotation, it can also be found in Loisy (though not quite at the chapter and page Camus indicates), and the reader discovers that Loisy's point was somewhat different from Camus': "Elle institua donc des initiations très *saintes* où seraient représentées par des images, des allégories et par des scènes figurées les souffrances de *jadis*." [39]

As to the opening chapter of the essay, "Evangelical Christianity," it is a melting pot of various sources. For the first section, "Evangelical Christian themes," Camus is especially indebted to P. de Labriolle's two important works on the early Christian era, *La Réaction paienne*, and *Histoire de la Literature Latine Chrétienne.* [40] Section two, a brief study of the major figures of evangelical Christianity, is gathered almost entirely from J. Tixeront's accurate but somewhat inadequate textbook on early Christian dogma. [41] Section three, on the obstacles to, and the reasons for, the evolution of Gospel Christianity, is a mosaic of information, nearly every piece of which might be found either in Tixeront, M.-P. Puech, or Labriolle. [42] Throughout

---

[37] *Ibid.*

[38] A. Loisy, *op. cit.*, p. 72. Camus fails to explain the meaning of this obscure reference.

[39] *Ibid.*, Chapter V, p. 141, and not IV, p. 139, as Camus indicates.

[40] *Métaphysique Chrétienne* ..., in *Essais*, pp. 1232-39; cf. P. Labriolle, *La Réaction Paienne* (Paris, 1934), esp. pp. 14-15, and also pp. 234 and 271; *Histoire de la littérature Latine Chrétienne* (Paris, 1920), esp. pp. 25-26 and p. 402.

[41] *Métaphysique Chrétienne*, in *Essais*, pp. 1239-45. Cf. J. Tixeront, *Histoire des Dogmes dans l'Antiquité Chrétienne*, Vol. I (Paris, 1915), esp. pp. 119-120, 128-129, and 148-162.

[42] *Métaphysique Chrétienne*, in *Essais*, pp. 1245-1250. Cf. M-P. Puech, *Les Apologistes Grecs du IIᵉ Siècle à Notre Ere* (Paris, 1912); J. Tixeront, *op. cit.*; also Labriolle, works cited in footnote 40.

the chapter, Camus is either delinquent or erratic in indicating his references, and he quite regularly succumbs to his unscholarly habit of giving impressive quotations from primary sources which he quite probably never consulted.

What of the accuracy of Camus' analysis of the historical encounter between Hellenism and Christianity, and of the factors that preceded and nurtured it? Since he relied so heavily on the findings and conclusions of first-rate historians, he surely cannot be accused of having made intuitive or groundless generalizations. His nearly total reliance upon secondary sources is in itself a guarantee of solidity, if not of originality. But scholars are notorious for contradicting one another, and themselves, particularly when they are dealing with such a vast and explosive subject as the encounter of Hellenism with Christianity. The major criticism one might make against Camus' analysis of this important period is that he does not seem fully to have realized to what extent his scholarly sources disagreed in their fundamental premises. For such ultra-rationalists as Rougier and Bréhier, the Greek universe was totally intelligible, scientific, and harmonious; and it clashed radically with Christianity, the success of which they considered harmful to philosophy as well as science. [43] From a viewpoint favorable to Christianity, the Catholic historian Pierre de Labriolle agreed with Bréhier and Rougier that Hellenism and Christianity were opposed on a number of vital points — Creation *ex nihilo*, the ideas of Providence, Sin, Grace, Redemption — but he considered the historical ascendancy of Christianity as a phenomenon that is at once dynamic, original, and divinely intended. [44] From a hostile perspective, Ernest Havet's four-volume history of the origins of Christianity is based upon an assumption diametrically opposed to those of Bréhier, Rougier, and Labriolle: that nothing about Christianity was original, that every single one of its themes had been prefigured in Hellenism. [45]

---

[43] Rougier, *Celse*, p. xx: "La Grèce proclame le primat de l'intelligence: la science, le rationalisme, le classicisme .... Le Chrétien ne voit dans la nature que bassesse, corruption, occasion de péché." Cf. Emile Bréhier, *Histoire de la Philosophie*, Vol. I (Paris, 1934), pp. 489-90: "Le cosmos des Grecs est un monde pour ainsi dire sans histoire, un ordre éternel .... L'idée inverse ... a été impossible avant que le christianisme ne vienne bouleverser le cosmos des Hellènes...."

[44] P. de Labriolle, *La Réaction Païenne*, pp. 14-15.

[45] Ernest Havet, *Le Christianisme et ses Origines*, Vol. I (Paris, 1871), p. vi: "Car c'est précisément ce que je me propose d'établir, que le Christia-

And behind this already dissonant chorus of scholars, Camus — had his ear been fine enough — might have heard the strident if prophetic voice of Niezsche crying "a pox on both your houses, for Greek rationalism and Christian moralism are part and parcel of the same Socratic disease."

Despite his prudent warning, at the start of *Christian Metaphysics*, about the arbitrariness of talking about a "Greek spirit," as opposed to a "Christian spirit," Camus might have noticed either that his sources called for a number of more acute distinctions, or that the term "Hellenism" remains undefinable. As it appears in *Christian Metaphysics*, his conception of Hellenism is afflicted with the very arbitrariness he would have wished to eschew. In a sense, Camus was the victim of his uncritical attitude towards his sources: his general vision of the Greek universe had been bequeathed to him by an ardent German Hellenist who loathed philologists, as well as by serene French philologists who looked askance at intuitive scholarship. It would have taken a most ingenious conductor to induce such a motley chorus to sing in unison. Camus had neither the taste nor the experience required for such an adventure of the mind; and, though he did attain a more sophisticated comprehension of Greek culture in his later years, his total vision of Hellenism and Christianity is obscured by ambiguities and contradictions much like those that remain in the opening chapter of *Christian Metaphysics*.

* * *

Camus had concluded his essay much in line with Harnack's thesis that, by the beginning of the fifth century, the chronic Hellenization of Christianity had reached its virtual completion. It seems pertinent to ask why the fusion of Greek and Christian values, which the young Camus had presented as historically evident, remained to him a philosophical impossibility. On what grounds do Hellenism and Christianity remain, from Camus' perspective, irrevocably opposed? The issues on which they differ in the twentieth century are somewhat different from those that elicited either the sarcasm or the

---

nisme est beaucoup plus hellénique qu'il n'est juif." (Camus cites Havet's four-volume study in the bibliography of *Christian Metaphysics*, in *Essais*, p. 1312.)

anxiety of pagan apologists such as Celsus, Porphyry, or Julian. It is
not the Christian dogmas of Creation *ex nihilo,* bodily resurrection,
or even Sin, Redemption or Grace — considered as abstract proposi-
tions — that kept Camus from attempting to reconcile his Greek heart
with his Christian sensibility. In modern terms, the conflict is both
more concrete and more profound; and with his fondness for antitheses, Camus might have summarized it aphoristically as follows: Hellenism is rebellious, whereas Christianity is resigned; Hellenism is
esthetic, whereas Christianity is moral; Hellenism is tragic, whereas
Christianity is dramatic; Hellenism is "natural," whereas Christianity
is "historical."

Camus might never have stated the first antithesis so simple-
mindedly. To begin with, he was never so naive as to pretend that
revolt was a Greek invention. The concept of evil, by his own admission, is an infrequent occurrence in Greek literature, as is, indeed, the
concept of sin. Long before the Judaic Satan had appeared in literature, however, the Greek genius had already dramatized the myth
of a human rebel's defiance of the gods. Prometheus' struggle against
death, his love for mankind, his messianic ambitions, his thirst for
justice, all the characteristics of modern rebellion are present in the
play of Aeschylus. [46] The original model of metaphysical rebellion in
Western literature is, then, unquestionably, a Greek one: "Alas!" cries
Prometheus, "see the injustices I have to endure!" [47]

Such models, however, are very rare, principally because metaphysical rebellion presupposes a simplified view of the universe, which
the Greeks could not possibly have. In their cosmos, the gods were
never lined up on one side, and men on the other. There were degrees
leading from one camp to the other. It would never have occurred
to them to oppose innocence to guilt, or to summarize history as a
struggle between good and evil. The Greeks were of the opinion that
there are more errors than crimes, and that the only definitive crime
is *húbris.* Even when they must act "excessively," for example, the
Greek tragic heroes never go so far as to consider themselves as
entirely innocent, nor do they push their defiance of the gods to the
point of blasphemy or vindictiveness. Like Prometheus, Achilles,

---

[46] *HR,* in *Essais,* p. 438.
[47] *Ibid.*

Oedipus and Antigone realize that to rebel against nature or destiny amounts to rebelling against oneself. [48]

While Greek literature posits degrees leading from the human to the divine order, these degrees are infallibly of a rational nature. From the Presocratics to Plotinus, Greek philosophers were convinced that the wise man could, by dint of his own effort, raise himself to the estate of the gods. In Plato, as in Plotinus and the Neoplatonic tradition, the philosopher "returns within himself," there to find the entire hierarchy of Being. A concentrated life is the indispensable prerequisite to a discovery of the highest Good. "Without always admitting the fact," Camus once declared, "Greek philosophy made of the wise man an equal of God. God was nothing other than the highest science . . ." [49] There are, to be sure, intermediate degrees in the philosopher's ascent from the world of sense to the world of ideas; but the gods cannot make the ascent less rugged than nature wills it, nor can they bestow wisdom upon those from whom nature has withheld it. The philosopher must, as it were, go it alone.

The belief that God was accessible to a privileged segment of thinking humanity was a Greek idea. The belief that God shared the same destiny as humanity, including its mortality, so as to narrow the chasm separating Him from mankind, is a Christian idea. The radical opposition between these conceptions explains the difference between the Greek and the Christian response to evil. The Greek, if he holds the gods responsible for evil, can protest, provided his defiance does not transgress the boundaries set by nature. The Christian must stifle his temptation to protest, remembering that God Himself, in the person of his only-begotten Son, chose freely to submit to the same evils as mankind. Christianity, therefore, has painted the harsh figure of the Judaic God in softer colors with the introduction of a mediator between God and man: "Christ came to resolve two major problems, evil and death, which are precisely the problems that preoccupy the rebel. His solution consisted, first, in experiencing them. The man-god suffers, too — with patience. Evil and death can no longer be entirely imputed to Him since He suffers and dies." [50]

---

[48] *Ibid.*, p. 439.

[49] *Métaphysique Chrétienne,* in *Essais,* p. 1226.

[50] *HR,* in *Essais,* p. 444. Cf. A. Camus, *The Rebel,* trans. by Anthony Bower New York, 1967), p. 32. I have used Bower's translation in quoting some of the longer passages.

For centuries, Camus remarks, the Christian answer to evil remained the only one. "Each time a solitary cry of rebellion was uttered, the answer came in the form of an even more terrible suffering. In that Christ had suffered, and had suffered voluntarily, suffering was no longer unjust and all pain was necessary. In one sense, Christianity's bitter intuition and legitimate pessimism concerning human behavior is based on the assumption that over-all injustice is as satisfying to man as total justice." [51] For centuries, Christians have responded to every protest against evil by pointing to the historical precedent of the crucifixion. The only cure to the evils that are suffered in history, they say, is to be found outside history. [52] Thus Christianity has in fact justified every form of historical injustice. It is, first and moremost, Camus argues, "a philosophy of injustice." Quoting the Christian poet, Gertrude von le Fort, he adds, "The world was not saved for those who are on the side of innocence . . . . It was saved by the painful agony of innocence." [53]

In its very attempt to humanize the figure of God, then, Christianity has fed the fires of metaphysical revolt. Camus argues convincingly, howbeit paradoxically, that the real history of rebellion is contemporaneous with Christianity. In asserting that the universe was created, and is governed, by a personal, providential, and benevolent God, Christianity necessarily hardened the determination of those rebels who would have no part of it. The Greek gods could not be held accountable for the cruel fantasies of the material world, since they were not its creators, and were themselves subjected to the eternal limitations of Necessity. As Creator and Maintainer of life, the Christian God must assume the responsibility for everything that goes on. The historical incarnation of the Son only makes the presence of evil more scandalous.

* * *

A second ambiguous heritage bequeathed by Christianity was the idea of history, a sign of contradiction insofar as it conflicts with the Greek concept of Nature. The conflict did not arise in a day, or

---

[51] *HR*, in *Essais*, p. 445. Cf. *The Rebel*, trans. by Anthony Bower, p. 34.
[52] *HR*, in *Essais*, p. 706.
[53] A. Camus, "Remarque sur la Révolte," (*L'Existence*, 1945), in *Essais*, p. 1690.

even a generation. Like Nietzsche, Bréhier, Chestov, Spengler, and Berdiaev (among the "Hellenic" sources he knew best), Camus considered it a historical truism that the Greeks had no sense of history. "The Greeks, a happy people, have no history," he writes in his *Notebooks,* punning perhaps unconsciously on the French phrase "pas d'histoire," which can mean both "no history" and "no troubles." [54] In its initial encounter with Hellenism, he argues in *The Rebel,* Christianity began by adopting the Greek idea of Nature; but is was simultaneously introducing into Western thought the belief in a personal destiny of the soul, in a beginning and an end of the world, thereby sowing the seeds of historical thinking. Towards the end of the Middle Ages, Christianity "squandered its Mediterranean heritage," concentrated its ambitions on temporal power at the expense of nature, significantly replaced the Romanesque by the Gothic, and slowly broke its historic alliance with Hellenism. For a time, the Christian idea of the immortal soul provided a metphysical fixity in Western thinking, which had heretofore been the prerogative of Nature. But towards the end of the Eighteenth Century, when rationalist criticism began to deny both the supernatural origins of Christianity and the traditional idea of the soul, History remained dangerously alone as the sole criterion of truth. [55]

History, therefore, is an invention as Christian as Nature is Greek; [56] and, in this regard, Christianity is far closer to Marxism than to Hellenism. "It is a Christian idea," asserts Camus, echoing Karl Jaspers, "to consider human history as a unique phenomenon." [57] And he continues:

> The Christians were the first to consider human life and the course of events as a history that is unfolding from a fixed beginning toward a definite end, in the course of which man achieves his salvation or earns his punishment. The philosophy of history springs from a Christian representation which is surprising to a Greek mind. The Greek idea of evolution has nothing in common with our idea of historical evolution. The difference between the two is the difference between a circle and a straight line. The Greeks imagined the history of the world as cyclical. Aristotle, to give a definite example,

---

[54] *Carnets,* I, p. 100.
[55] *HR,* in *Essais,* pp. 594-95.
[56] *Métaphysique Chrétienne,* in *Essais,* p. 1228 and 1309.
[57] *HR,* in *Essais,* p. 594.

did not believe that the time in which he was living was subsequent to the Trojan War. Christianity was obliged, in order to penetrate the Mediterranean world, to Hellenize itself, and its doctrine then became more flexible. But its originality lay in introduction into the ancient world two ideas that had never before been associated: the idea of history and the idea of punishment....

... The love of the ancients for the cosmos was completely unknown to the first Christians, who, moreover, awaited with impatience an imminent end of the world. Hellenism, in association with Christianity, then produces the admirable efflorescence of the Albigensian heresy on the one hand, and on the other Saint Francis. But with the Inquisition and the destruction of the Albigensian heresy, the Church again parts company with the world and with beauty, and gives back to history its pre-eminence over nature.... The delicate equilibrium between humanity and nature, man's consent to the world, which gives ancient thought its distinction and its refulgence, was first shattered for the benefit of history by Christianity.... From the moment that the divinity of Christ is denied, or that, thanks to the efforts of German ideology, He only symbolizes the man-god, the concept of mediation disappears and a Judaic world reappears.... Marx, from this point of view, is the Jeremiah of the god of history and the Saint Augustine of the revolution. [58]

Since Christianity was the first to turn its back to nature and the world so as to enslave man in the prison of history, it must be held responsible for the aberrations of modern historicism. "Communism is a logical consequence of Christianity." [59] "Christianity explains bolshevism." [60] Both Christianity and Marxism have "slandered" Greek values. Both base their message upon a revelation, which in the case of the former occurs at the beginning of history, and in the case of the latter at the end. Both these religions sacrifice the present to the future. Both live in the expectation of a *parousia* that will justify both historical suffering and historical crime. Neither is excessively embarrassed by the contradictions of its gospels or the excesses of its churches. [61] For Camus, Marxism is little other than Christianity deprived of its mystery.

---

[58] *Ibid.*, pp. 594-95. Cf. *The Rebel*, trans. by A. Bower, pp. 189-91.
[59] *Carnets*, II, p. 164.
[60] *Ibid.*, p. 235.
[61] *Ibid.*, pp. 240 and 336.

The twentieth century, with its totalitarian religions spawned by the failure of Christianity, has "rehabilitated the order of Grace without God," and, in a vertiginous about-face, has restored the mystical body in its most despicable forms. [62] "We live in a kind of Middle Ages without the consolations of Grace," declares Camus, in one of his more despondent moments. And in *The Exile of Helen*, a moving essay on the disappearance of Greek values in the modern world, he exclaims: "We have exiled beauty. The Greeks took up arms to defend it .... Greek thought never exaggerated anything, whether sacred or rational. The Greeks found a place for everything, and counterbalanced light with shadow. Europe, on the other hand, in pursuing its conquest of totality, is the child of excess." [63] Like the barbarians, whom the Greeks fought to the death at Salamis, modern Europe has placed history on the throne of God and is slowly become a theocracy. All one need do, in order to measure the difference that separates modern Europe from the Greeks, is to read Hegel, the only modern rival of Plato, who pretends that the modern city is the only place where the spirit can take consciousness of itself. The modern world has been cut off from nature, and plunged into history; but "history cannot explain the cosmos that came before it, nor beauty, which is above it .... While in Plato one can find everything — irrationality, reason, and myth — our philosophers give us nothing except irrationality and reason, since they have closed their eyes to the rest." [64]

Christianity made itself responsible for the exile of Helen when it began to pretend that the tragedy of the soul was more important than the contemplation of the universe. But Christianity at least had the merit of maintaining a certain fixity, as it declared the soul, a spiritual substance, its point of reference. Since the death of God, unfortunately, there are no points of reference except will, unchecked by reason, and history, unchecked by nature. Today, moral values

---

[62] The responsibility of Christianity for modern historicism is demonstrated, according to Camus, by the Christian "flavor" of nineteenth-century historical and social thinking, particularly that of Hegel (*HR*, in *Essais*, p. 550), Comte, "The Saint Paul of his new religion" (*Ibid.*, p. 600), and Feuerbach (*Ibid.*, p. 553). It is significant, Camus remarks, that the clerical Joseph de Maistre is hostile to Greece (*Ibid.*, p. 598).

[63] "L'Exil d'Hélène," in *Essais*, p. 853.

[64] *Ibid.*, pp. 854-55.

do not antecede action, they are a product of it. "Heracleitus once described excess as a conflagration. Well, the conflagration is now out of control." [65]

The only answer to the problem is to take up arms to save Helen, for, in a sense, she has never died within us. Historical absolutism, Camus warns, will inevitably clash with the invincible claims of nature. The key to the modern dilemma resides, perhaps, in Goethe's version of the myth of Helen. Goethe married Faust (modern titanism) with Helen (eternal beauty), and gave them a son named Euphorion. The modern Faust would, it seems, like to beget Euphorion without the intervention of Helen; but, instead of a beautiful son, he can produce nothing except a laboratory monster. The tragedy of our age is not that it is Faustian, but that Faust thinks he can do without Helen. "Goethe, who had his occasional moments of prophecy, had Euphorion die, for he was too beautiful to live in this unhappy world. For myself, I think that whether Euphorion lives or dies depends entirely upon us." [66]

* * *

Camus occasionally expressed the conflict between Hellenism and Christianity in terms of the Nietzschean antithesis between an esthetic and a moral justification of the world. The terms of this antithesis, like those I have been discussing, might be replaced by the terms "static" and "dynamic." In a universe that is in every detail, and at every moment identical to itself, the supreme human activity must be either artistic or scientific, according to whether one's vision of that universe is Heracleitean or Platonic. For most Greek philosophers, action was, to use the words of Plotinus, "a diminution of contemplation." In a historical universe, on the other hand, the supreme human value is not contemplation, but, as Goethe puts it, "the deed."

"The Greeks," as Camus repeatedly asserted, "justified the world in esthetic terms." [67] This is not to say that they had no moral sense, but simply that they considered the search for truth inseparable from the love of beauty. All that is beautiful and harmonious in nature is considered "good." All that is evil, or ugly, or grotesque, is "bad."

---

[65] *Ibid.*

[66] "Remarque sur la Révolte," in *Essais*, p. 1711.

[67] *Métaphysique Chrétienne*, in *Essais*, p. 1225.

Evil might, therefore, be considered a prevarication against nature rather than an offense against God. These formulas, however simplified, provide an accurate summary of what Camus meant by "Greek estheticism."

With the advent of Christianity, esthetics and morals tend to become separate spheres. "To see, and to see on this earth" is no longer a sufficient initiation to the divine mysteries, and contemplation of the universe is not a guarantee of salvation. [68] A creature can be simultaneously beautiful and evil: indeed, as in the case of Lucifer or Jezabel, the more evil they are the more beautiful they tend to be. A body, whether natural or artificial, can be both esthetically attractive and displeasing to God: a Pagan idol, for example, or an "immoral" work of art. On the other hand, the Christian scheme makes it possible to have an ugly body and a "beautiful soul." Man's life being essentially a spiritual odyssey, an *itinerarium mentis ad Deum,* it matters little whether the Christian achieves a perfect harmony of his natural forces — such a harmony might even be a hindrance to salvation — but whether he obeys God and avoids sin. Indeed, it might even be necessary to do violence to one's nature, in order to obey the will of God. Nature can be justified only by the hidden truth it conceals. The Christian must discern in it the "symbol of hidden things." The world of sense is neither self-sufficient, nor self-justifying. Its value resides in the absence that it reveals. Camus' aphorism is a most perceptive one: "For the Greek," he suggests, "nature is a force that must be obeyed; for the Christian, as for the Marxist, it is a force that must be overcome." [69]

The further removed Christian thought becomes from its Greek sources, the more marked its tendency to sum up the course of history in terms of good and evil. Heretical Christianity, in this regard, provides a better example than does orthodoxy. The Gnostics, for instance, consider universal history as a struggle between the superior and the maleficent deity: theirs is a world wherein the tragedy of the soul is daily being enacted, as on a stage. [70] As for Camus, he feels little inclination towards the moral world view of Christianity,

---

[68] "Noces à Tipasa," in *Essais,* p. 57: "Aux mystères d'Eleusis il suffisait de contempler [pour être initié]."

[69] *HR,* in *Essais,* p. 488.

[70] *Métaphysique Chrétienne,* in *Essais,* p. 1265. Cf. *infra,* chapter three.

whether orthodox or heretical. The reduction of the cosmos into moral categories — humility, sin, corruption of nature, repentance — he calls "a perpetual attempt to present man with an unfavorable reflection of himself." [71] The moral outlook conspires to make him turn his eyes away from the present, while the esthetic outlook characteristically refuses to look "away," or "beyond." The moral outlook declares that sin is an excessive attachment to the world. The esthetic outlook responds that "the real sin, the only sin I am capable of understanding, is to turn one's eyes away from the implacable grandeur of this life." [72] The Christian, in sum, like his Marxist counterpart, can allow himself to tame nature, master it, look beyond it, or repress it; he can never maintain that nature justifies itself.

* * *

In literature the difference between the esthetic and the moral points of view is best illustrated by tragedy and drama. The Christian universe, Camus claims, is fundamentally dramatic, but never tragic. [73] This does not mean that a Christian civilization is incapable of producing tragedies: the Elizabethan stage, the Spanish theatre of the *Siglo de Oro* offer irrefutable evidence to the contrary. The tragedies of the Renaissance period, however, were the creations of a period during which the individual, with his need for self-assertion and power, entered into conflict with the accepted, if declining, values of his civilization. Towards the end of the Middle Ages, in fact, Western civilization witnessed the most fertile tragic period since Aeschylus and Sophocles. The common characteristic of both these ages, separated as they were by two millenia, is that they marked a transition between what Camus calls "cosmic forms of thinking," and "individualistic or rationalistic forms." Between Aeschylus and Euripides, there occurs an evolution quite similar to the one that links the Presocratic thinkers to Socrates. Analogously, between Shakespeare and Corneille, the obscure and mystery-filled universe of medieval times has been transformed into a universe wherein universal values are

---

[71] *Carnets,* II, p. 16: "Depuis 2000 ans, l'homme s'est vu présenter une image humiliée de lui-même."

[72] "L'Eté à Alger," in *Essais,* p. 76: "Il y a des mots que je n'ai jamais bien compris, comme celui de péché . . . ." etc.

[73] *L'Avenir de la Tragédie,* in *TRN,* p. 1700.

asserted and upheld by dint of human will and reason.[74] A tragic age, therefore, is one during which man, in attempting to disengage himself from the ancient structures of a essentially religious civiliza- tion, discovers that he is torn between the old values and the new, which he is as yet unable to couch in satisfactory forms of expression.[75]

If such seem to be the characteristics of a tragic era, what, then, is tragedy? It seems to be man's protest against a divine order, whether personified by a God or symbolized by a social organism. The inten- sity of the tragedy is proportionate to the legitimacy of the revolt and to the necessity for the existence of the order.[76] Neither the hero nor the order is entirely innocent or guilty. In a drama, on the other hand, everyone knows where legitimacy lies. While in a drama, "one man alone is just and justifiable," all of the tragic figurae can be justified, yet none of them is just.[77]

While it is possible, therefore, to conceive of a tragedy being writ- ten during a Christian civilization, it is impossible to imagine a Christian tragedy. In a tragic universe, evil is a mute and irresolute force, difficult to analyze or isolate. The tragic conflict might con- ceivably be resolved, but the mechanism that produced it, or set it in motion, cannot be explained entirely. Christianity, on the other hand, has offered a conceptual explanation for the presence of evil and suffering: they are due either to the presence of Satan, or to the sin of Adam and his descendants, or to the consequences of that sin (such as living in a corruptible flesh). Total goodness and total in- nocence are attributes that the Christian can ascribe only to God: "Nemo bonus, nisi unus Deus."[78] There can be no "tragic" conflict between the Christian and the divine order, since God alone is just, and next to Him, man is as nothing:

> Since the Christian divine order leaves no place for dispu- tation, but merely for sin and repentance, there can be no tragedy. There can at best be mystery, or parable, or what Spanish theatre calls "act of faith," or "sacramental act," namely, a spectacle wherein the one truth is solemnly pro- claimed. One might, therefore, imagine a religious drama,

---

[74] *Ibid.*
[75] *Ibid.*, p. 1701.
[76] *Ibid.*, p. 1704.
[77] *Ibid.*, p. 1703.
[78] *Mark* X: 18. Cf. *Métaphysique Chrétienne,* in *Essais,* p. 1234.

not a religious tragedy. This explains the silence of tragedy before the Renaissance. Medieval Christianity immersed man, the earth, and the entire universe, in the divine milieu. Consequently, the Christian universe allows for no tension between man and the divine principle. At best, it allows for ignorance, or the struggle involved in the renunciation of passion in order to embrace the spiritual life. Perhaps there was only one Christian tragedy in history, the one enacted on Mount Golgotha at that fleeting moment when Jesus cried: "My God! why hast thou forsaken me?" That moment of doubt, that moment alone, was enough to generate the ambiguity needed in a tragic situation. Thereafter, the divinity of Christ was no longer a matter of doubt. The Mass, which is a daily consecration of this divinity, is the finest illustration of religious theatre in our Western civilization: not a creation, but a repetition. [79]

* * *

With the possible exception of the first, the foregoing antitheses had to a large extent been suggested to Camus by some of his favorite philosophical sources. Of these, he had always leaned instinctively towards Nietzsche, Hegel, Chestov, Berdiaev, to name his evident preferences. Each was, in a sense, a child of Greece. Those, like Berdiaev and Chestov, who clearly preferred Judaic-Christian values to Hellenic, had never ceased to admire Greek culture, and had literally spent their lifetimes studying the implications of Christianity's encounter with Hellenism. Little wonder, then, that Camus' formulation of the ideological struggle between Hellenism and Christianity should reflect some of their main theses.

Camus had clearly found in Nietzsche a confirmation of his own instinctive resentment towards the Christian moral view. One remembers that, in his *Attempt at Self-Criticism* (1886), Nietzsche had hinted that his hostility towards the moral view of life could perhaps best be measured by his "prudent and hostile silence," throughout *The Birth of Tragedy*, towards Christianity, that "wildest variation on the theme of morality ever composed." [80] Nietzsche thought it impossible to imagine anything more antithetical to an esthetic inter-

[79] "L'Avenir de la Tragédie," in *TRN*, p. 1704.
[80] F. Nietzsche, *Essai d'Autocritique (1886)*, in *La Naissance de la Tragédie*, trans. by G. Bianquis (Paris, 1949), p. 133.

pretation of the world than Christian dogma, which, he claimed, relegates art to the estate of a beautiful lie.[81] In this "hostility" towards art, Nietzsche thought he could discern a raging malevolence towards life itself. "The universe and human existence," he cried, "can be justified only as esthetic phenomena!"[82]

Camus never felt the need to express his hostility towards the Christian moral view quite so stridently as Nietzsche, principally because, unlike Nietzsche (who never quite shook the preacher's son out of his system), he had always considered himself a pagan; nor did his hostility towards the moral view imply a rejection of such a wide variety of amenities as it did for Nietzsche, reason and happiness, for example. In the Nietzschean view, moralism was a veritable Pandora's box that had been built in Socrates' workshop, and into which had been thrown all the illusions that nourish those of us who do not have the fortune of being supermen: the principal illusion being that "reason leads to virtue, and that virtue leads to happiness." Socrates had built the box and forgotten to lock it; Jesus, Paul, and their followers had opened the lid.

Camus shared Nietzsche's hostility towards sin, which, he confessed, was a notion he had never quite understood; but he never considered sin as a "feminine, Semitic notion," whose counterpart was the "virile, Aryan" idea of crime.[83] (That particular antithesis is one for which Camus, though an ardent reader of Nietzsche, seems to have had little taste.) Unlike the German philosopher, Camus looked upon Socratic dialectics, moral intellectualism, and individual happiness as highly desirable, indeed rare achievements of the human spirit. "Men die," says Caligula, "and are not happy;" and to Camus, this seemed the supreme human tragedy. At times he seems to have sensed the danger involved in Nietzsche's Aryanized Hellenism, though he never took sharp issue with Nietzsche on this point. While he had a deep distaste for moral codes of behavior dictated "from the top of some Mount Sinai," he professed that, pace Nietzsche, the Socratic moral ideal is very much an integral part of Hellenism, and that even

---

[81] *Ibid.*: "toute vie repose sur l'apparence, l'art, l'illusion, l'optique, le perspectivisme nécessaire et l'erreur. Le christianisme, dès le principe, a été essentiellement le dégoût ... de vivre ...."

[82] *Ibid.*, p. 119: "l'existence et le monde ne sont justifiables qu'en tant que phénomènes esthétiques."

[83] F. Nietzsche, *La Naissance de la Tragédie* (Paris, 1949), chapter 9.

the values of pre-Socratic Greece are best served by keeping Socrates alive. It is, indeed, difficult to read *The Birth of Tragedy* without a mixture of irritation and apprehension: Nietzsche's dogmatic contention that the Greek moral sense was "the simple-minded invention of German philology," and that the primitive Greek instinct is the will to power and internecine destruction leaves one apprehensive about the fate of any Mediterranean idea that has the misfortune of entering an Aryan mind. [84]

Camus' antithesis between tragedy and drama, again, is an originally Nietzschean idea. Nietzsche did not think, for example, that Euripides' plays deserved the name of "tragedies," but of "dramatic epics," [85] the major innovation of Euripidean theatre being that dialogue takes precedence over music, that the hero is dramatically more important than the chorus, and that the intent of the play is to produce a moral catharsis within the spectator. "Let us," wrote Nietzsche, "consider the consequences of the Socratic theses: 'Virtue is knowledge ... a man sins out of ignorance ... the virtuous man is happy.' These three optimistic maxims constitute the death of tragedy. The virtuous hero must henceforth be a dialectician; and a visible, necessary link must relate virtue with conscience, faith with morality. The transcendent justice of Aeschylus degenerates into a flat and impertinent 'poetic justice,' with its customary *deus ex machina*." [86]

Camus' *Essay on Music*, published in 1932, is undoubtedly his earliest attempt to define tragedy in Nietzschean terms. [87] In an inaccurate summary of Nietzsche's thought, he defines Apollonianism as "the need to forget one's individuality and to identify with all of humanity." [88] Curiously enough, he describes the Dionysian instinct in almost identical terms: "a veritable drunkenness, whose effect is to

---

[84] F. Nietzsche, "Le Crépuscule des Faux Dieux," in *La Naissance de la Tragédie*, trans. by G. Bianquis, pp. 138-39: "J'apercevais leur instinct le plus fort, la volonté de puissance, je les voyais trembler devant la force indomptable de cet instinct, je voyais toutes leurs institutions naître de mesures de protection destinées à mettre chacun à l'abri des masses de *matière explosive* que le prochain portait en soi."

[85] F. Nietzsche, *La Naissance de la Tragédie*, trans. by G. Bianquis, chapter 12.

[86] *Ibid.*, chapter 14.

[87] "Essai sur la Musique," in *Essais*, pp. 1200-1203.

[88] *Ibid.*, p. 1201.

make us forget our very individuality." [89] These two instincts, adds Camus, "concur to make us forget the painful side of existence." The Greeks, torn as they were by political strife, ambition, jealousy, and violence, had a wider experience of pain than most peoples; and, since they were more prone to suffering, they "felt the horrors of life more cruelly," and made use of music and dancing in order to "remedy these savage horrors." [90]

The entire essay bears the mark of Camus' youthful and uncritical enthusiasm for Nietzsche. One senses that he has read *The Birth of Tragedy* with the ardor of a neophyte, and has swallowed the doctrine whole.

His lecture on *The Future of Tragedy* (1955) is a far better piece of scholarship. Though the essay still bears a Nietzschean earmark, Camus' own views are asserted far more vigorously. Gone is the classic, somewhat overused antithesis between the Apollonian and the Dionysiac; gone the somewhat tearful *rapport* between the Greeks' sense of tragedy and their "proneness to suffering;" gone, finally, the abstruse considerations on the function of music. Even this essay, however, continues to be guided by Nietzsche's historical scheme: between Aeschylus and Euripides there is an artistic decline, due in great part to Euripides' own ratiocinations. "Nietzsche was right," Camus admits, "in calling Socrates the gravedigger of tragedy." [91]

Camus' antithesis between tragedy and drama, in the same essay, is quite clearly a variant of the Nietzschean opposition between "theoretical thought" and "tragic vision." [92] His suggestion that an excessive dose of scientific rationalism is toxic to the spirit of tragedy could have been written by Nietzsche himself, as could the admonition that tragedy is not to be defined as a struggle of good against evil. Camus' positive definition of tragedy as "a conflict between individual and cosmic forces" would, however, seem to dissociate him from Nietzsche, who considered the very notion of conflict as decadent: conflict, argued

---

[89] *Ibid.*

[90] *Ibid.*, p. 1202. Cf. *La Naissance de la Tragédie,* chapter 25, "combien ce peuple a dû souffrir pour atteindre à tant de beauté." Camus' definition of music as the "expression d'un monde inconnaissable, monde d'essence spirituelle qui s'exprimerait d'une façon idéale," in the same essay (*Ibid.*, p. 1203) is a restatement of Nietzsche's idea that music represents the thing in itself rather than phenomena" (*La Naissance de la Tragédie,* chapter 16.)

[91] "L'Avenir de la Tragédie," in *TRN*, p. 1706.

[92] F. Nietzsche, *La Naissance de la Tragédie,* chapter 17.

Nietzsche, entails dialectics, and dialectics imply that someone is right and someone wrong. [93] It seems difficult, at first, not to agree with Nietzsche against Camus: how can one define tragedy as "conflict" without expecting moral judgments to be made, whether by the author, the chorus, or the personae?

Such, however, is perhaps Camus' most original hypothesis, in *The Future of Tragedy*: the dialectic of tragedy does not force the spectator to take sides. Tragic heroes can be both innocent and guilty (Antigone, Creon, Oedipus), and tragic conflicts might be described in moral categories without being resolved with a false serenity. It is false to say, for example, that Sophocles makes no moral judgments; but it is equally false to pretend that Sophocles ever "blames" anyone, dividing his universe between the good and the bad.

In the final analysis, *The Future of Tragedy* owes perhaps more to Chestov than to Nietzsche. Quoting Hegel, in *Le Pouvoir des Clefs* (one of Camus' most important sourcebooks), Chestov defines tragedy as follows: "In an authentic tragedy, two equally just and moral forces must meet. Such, in effect, was the destiny of Socrates. It was more than a personal, individual, romantic destiny; in it was revealed a general, morally tragic destiny, the tragedy of Athens, the tragedy of Greece. Two clashing prerogatives enter into conflict and mutually destroy one another; each is defeated, yet each is right with respect to the other. One of these forces is divine right, established custom . . . objective freedom. The other principle is . . . subjective truth. Such are the two conflicting principles in the life and the philosophy of Socrates." [94] The *Future of Tragedy* is a remarkable illustration of Camus' ability to make judicious use of his sources, while keeping them at a critical distance.

The precise source of Camus' antithesis between nature and history is impossible to circumscribe. With understandable differences in language and perspective, Hegel, Nietzsche, Chestov, Berdiaev, and Bréhier had each described the distinction, or the conflict, between Hellenism and Christianity as being that between nature and history. It seems doubtful, at the outset, whether any two of these scholars could have agreed on a common definition of terms. For Nietzsche,

---

[93] *Ibid.*

[94] Leon Chestov, *Le Pouvoir des Clefs*, translated from the Russian by B. Schloezer (Paris, 1927), pp. 224-25.

"nature" meant an eternal, living, cosmic reality, the only object worthy of the superior mind's consideration, the volcano of Empedocles, the "play" of Heracleitus. By "history," Nietzsche meant a sickness of the mind which, bequeathed to humanity by post-Socratic thought, had degenerated, during the Nineteenth Century, into the graveyard scholarship of the German historical school. For Berdiaev, the distinction between nature and history is much the same as the Pauline antithesis between "law" and "spirit," "necessity" and "grace." Chestov — quite at an antipode from Hegel — considers nature as the object of man's scientific and rational inquiries, while history, that enclosure of concrete, individual events, is the "really real," escaping as its does the philosopher's every attempt at universalization. Bréhier, finally, argued, in his *History of Philosophy,* that "nature" is almost synonymous with the Greek "cosmos," an eternal, static, totally intelligible reality; and that history is a Judeo-Christian concept introduced into the Western conceptual baggage, along with the ideas of Creation, Incarnation, and Salvation. [95]

Despite their divergences, however, Camus' sources are in evident agreement on three major premises: that the Greeks had no sense of history; that history is a Christian, or Judeo-Christian, invention; that history is dissociated from nature, and in conflict with it.

Of Camus' sources, it is Berdiaev, in his *The Meaning of History,* who had perhaps formulated the antithesis between nature and history in the most emphatic terms. Camus seems to have agreed with the historical scheme of this profound Christian writer, though he could agree with him on little else. The Greeks, according to Berdiaev, "had no notion of the historical process," since they "perceived the world esthetically as an accomplished and harmonious cosmos." They were, he argues, a conservative people: their values, traditions, and myths were firmly rooted in a distant past. The appearance of Christ had been, on the other hand, the culmination of a dynamic, futuristic

---

[95] Emile Bréhier, *Histoire de la Philosophie,* Vol. I, pp. 489-90. The contrast between history and nature appears, with wide differences of interpretation, in the following works (to mention only some of the sources Camus is certain to have read): Emile Bréhier, *Histoire de la Philosophie,* Vol. I (esp. pp. 489-90); G. F. W. Hegel, *Leçons sur la Philosophie de l'Histoire,* Paris, 1937; Leon Chestov, *Le Pouvoir des Clefs,* Paris, 1927, and *Les Révelations de la Mort,* Paris, 1923; F. Nietzsche, *La Naissance de la Tragédie,* Paris, 1949; N. Berdiaev, *Le Sens de l'Histoire,* Paris, 1948.

process that had begun with Abraham; it freed mankind from the dominion of nature and necessity, under which the Greeks had lived. The birth of Christ was, according to Berdiaev, a unique event, "having all the particularities and properties of that which is historical." [96]

Although it inaugurated the order of history, Christianity continued to be enlivened and enriched by Greek philosophy, to which it owes its metaphysics and its sense of beauty. Christian historicism did, however, destroy man's sense of union with nature, thereby giving an indirect impetus to the development of technology and science, which remained an impossibility so long as human life was grounded upon a mythical conception of nature. Liberation from nature enabled the Christian to deepen his interior life, to wage in the arena of his own soul a heroic struggle that would bring an end to his slavery and a revelation of the "new man." "To forge a new image of man on the model of the new Adam, it was necessary to turn away from nature, while man in the ancient world was a reflection of the old Adam who . . . had allowed himself to lapse into an inferior and elementary nature . . . . Christianity was the first to proclaim the infinite value of the human soul, to which all the kingdoms of the world cannot be compared . . . . Its struggle against the powers of nature gave birth to the Christian dualism of nature and soul . . . . [Such a dualism] generates a dynamic principle . . . without which history would be impossible, for the subject would then remain anchored in the object." [97] Throughout the history of Christianity, there remains a residue of longing for Greek beauty; such a nostalgia, however, must remain forever hopeless, as the rift driven by the Christian conscience between the closed, immanent world of Hellenism and the infinite, transparent world of Christianity cannot be healed within the limitations of a historical culture. [98]

Camus' statement of the problem of history and nature is so similar to Berdiaev's as to appear virtually identical. Like the author of *The Meaning of History*, be argues: that the Greeks lived during a period of pre-historical, mythical consciousness; that Christianity is, by its very nature, hostile towards nature, which it considers either

---

[96] N. Berdiaev, *Le Sens de l'Histoire*, pp. 32-33; p. 92.
[97] *Ibid.*, p. 101.
[98] *Ibid.*, p. 116.

as a source of organic necessity, or of temptation and sin; that, in artistic terms, the substitution of history to nature was historically illustrated by the substitution of Gothic art (with its vertical *élan* towards infinity) for the harmony and the order of classicism; that there remains throughout the history of Christianity a certain nostalgia for Hellenic forms, to which Catholic Christianity, with its taste for contemplation and liturgical decoration, gives a particular expression; that Christianity is remotely responsible for the promotion of science and technology, as it looks upon nature as a source that must be dominated or controlled; that Marxism, and other forms of immanent historicism, have inherited their messianic drive from Judaism and Christianity.

On a fundamental article, Camus and Berdiaev are in total disagreement: Berdiaev, a Christian, always speaks of history as a transcendent, spiritual reality, the focus of divine activity within the Church and within time. Camus cannot prevent himself from considering history as a totally immanent reality which, left to its own devices, crushes everything in its path, like Juggernaut's car. He has, as it were, turned Berdiaev's analysis upon its head. While Berdiaev accuses modern scientism and historicism of being "acts of insurrection" against all that is truly historical, Camus estimates that modern historicism is a predictable, if tragic consequence of Christianity's millenial struggle to overcome nature. [99] Berdiaev insists repeatedly that a return to the sacred, i.e., Christian sense of history is necessary if the historical order is to have "messianic and eschatological justification." [100] Camus retorts that historical dynamism is destructive *in itself,* unless it is counterpoised by "la nature, avec ses anciennes exigences." [101]

Camus' antithesis between nature and history, then, is the product, curiously enough, of a Christian historical scheme. One might legitimately ask whether Berdiaev, for a Christian, does not oppose nature and history too neatly, or whether his idea of nature, in particular, is not faintly tinged with Gnosticism, as it frequently tends

---

[99] *Ibid.,* p. 100: "Tout paradoxal que cela puisse paraître, il me semble que seul le christianisme a rendu possibles la science de la nature et la technique positive .... Pourtant, bien qu'elle en soit un des points d'aboutissement, la conception mecaniste a fini par se dresser contre le christianisme."

[100] *Ibid.,* p. 213.

[101] *HR,* in *Essais,* p. 702.

to be among theologians of Eastern Christianity. For one might argue, in Christian terms, that the Incarnation of Christ should have reduced nature to the estate either of an abstraction or of an anachronism. For the Christian, who believes he lives in a divine milieu, nature and grace can be distinguished, as indeed can nature and history. But how can the distinction be anything other than a mental operation? For theologians of the Western Church, such as Augustine, "nature" is a concept meant to designate man's praeternatural state of perfection before the fall: an ideal state, therefore, or, at best a pre-historical state, as the fall of man represents, as it were, "the first event of the era of Grece." [102] For a thinker like Aquinas, "nature" refers to that reality which is the specific object of rational investigation. This, again, is an abstraction, since, in concrete fact, nature cannot be separated from supernature, as philosophy is a distinct, but not a separate pursuit from theology. [103]

It is misleading of Berdiaev, therefore, to underscore the Christian's "struggle to overcome" nature, or to "master" it, or to "liberate himself" from its clutches. This is acceptable phraseology to the Christian only if it means that he must correct whatever prevents

---

[102] The full meaning of "nature" in Augustine is a problem far too complex to settle in a sentence or a footnote. Let it suffice, for the present purpose to state that nature "as God had intended it" existed only before the fall of Adam; nature "after the fall" continues to be good, although sin detracts from the relative perfection it enjoyed in the prelapsal state; in sinning against God, therefore, man (the only creature, along with the angels, who is capable of sinning), is harming his own nature. Only before the fall of Adam, in any case, is it possible to speak of nature in the pure state. After the fall, nature can be rationally distinguished from grace, but is concretely inseparable from it. See, for example, *The City of God*, trans. by Marcus Dods (Random House, 1950), Book XIX, ch. 13-15, pp. 691-93: "And therefore there is a nature in which evil does not or even cannot exist [i.e. God]; but there cannot be a nature in which there is no good. Hence not even the nature of the devil himself is evil, in so far as it is nature; but it was made evil by being perverted.... God then, the most wise Creator and most just Ordainer of all natures, who placed the human race upon earth as its greatest ornament, imparted to men some good things adapted to this life.... This is prescribed by the order of nature: it is thus that God has created man."

[103] Frederick Copleston, S. J., *A History of Philosophy*, Vol. II, *Medieval Philosophy, Part II* (Image Books, 1950), p. 35: "This distinction [between the natural and supernatural ends of man] .... is not a distinction between two ends which correspond to two mutually exclusive orders, the one supernatural, the other that of 'pure nature': *it is a distinction between two orders of knowledge and activity in the same concrete human being*."

nature from being fully, and authentically, itself. It is (from the point of view of one who is accustomed to think in Augustinian and Thomistic terms) far more in keeping with the essence of Christianity to consider history, in its authentic, sacred sense, as a fulfillment of nature, or as an elevation of nature to a new level of reality and meaning. Such is my own view of the alleged opposition between nature and history, which I can not prevent myself from considering an artificial problem, or an intellectual diversion.

Camus' failure to understand the above distinctions, or his understandable ignorance of them, accounts for his tendency to view Christianity through a Gnostic optic. [104] Had he been misled by Berdiaev into thinking that Christianity is, in its very essence, hostile towards nature? Was he willfully beguiled by his instinctive admiration for the "catharic," anti-natural modes of Christianity into thinking that Christian dualism entails a necessary repudiation of natural values? Whatever his reasons may have been, it is simply erroneous to think that Christianity has made the concepts of nature and history mutually exclusive. The historical dynamism bequeathed to Western thought by Christianity, far from destroying the Greek idea of nature, might have intensified man's love for "a universe that sings the praises of God." The modern split between nature and history might not have been due to Christianity at all. It may, in fact, be argued that the one Western tradition that has continued to consider nature as a source of beauty, contemplation, and praise, is Christianity itself. Curiously enough, Christianity may be the only living Western ideology that has kept Hellenic values alive; and, though this paradox would never have won Camus' approval, it bears deeper investigation . . . .

* * *

One of Camus' infortunate *idées fixes* was to make Christianity remotely or immediately responsible for the ills of the modern era,

---

[104] There is an important, if fine distinction between the Christian view that nature, though a perfectible creation, can be an inducement to evil, and the Gnostic view that it is an intrinsically evil substance. Berdiaev, however severe in his attitude towards nature (see for example *Le Sens de l'Histoire*, p. 101) holds the former view while most of Camus' objections to Christian pessimism might more accurately be directed towards the latter view.

then to offer solutions that coincide in almost every detail with Christian thought. "I value only those elements of Christianity that are close to Hellenism," he once told Jean Grenier, [105] without realizing, perhaps, that the areas of agreement were far wider than he explicitly admitted. Consider their mythical structures, for example: both the episode of Eden and the myth of Prometheus seem to suggest an identical truth, that "man had the power of becoming equal to God, and that God was afraid of him, and kept him in subjection." It is both a Greek and a Christian idea to suggest that the gods are jealous. [106] As for the cross, it is not merely a Christian, but a Mediterranean symbol. [107] The abysmal sadness of Sisyphus, as he sets once again his shoulder against the rock, recalls the despair of Christ at Gethsemani. [108] Christ is the victim of the Christian mysteries, like the Dionysus of the Orphic rites; and, at Eleusis, Zeus is united with Demeter, as the Spirit is united with the Virgin. [109]

Though Camus repeatedly asserted that his morals were Greek, his ethical ideals frequently coincide with those of the Mount. Like Christ (and Socrates), he senses that the "true meaning of life" is to be discovered in leading a life of poverty, among humble people. [110] He notices at San Marco that Franciscan asceticism has a great deal in common with the "Greek" nakedness of the young bathers on Algerian beaches: "If they renounce everything, they do so in favor of a 'greater' life, and not of 'another' life.... I should convert myself to such renunciation, were it not already my religion." [111]

Poverty and nakedness entail a curious (and perhaps unfulfilled) taste for asceticism. Camus writes with astonishing frequency about the "absolute necessity" for sexual chastity. Many of his remarks on the subject, particularly in the *Notebooks,* betray a monastic, almost Manichean attitude towards the flesh. "Abandon all pretense, and strive towards a dual liberation: from money, and from your own vanity and cowardice.... " [112] "When asceticism is voluntary... [it

---

[105] Jean Grenier, *Albert Camus,* p. 137.
[106] *Carnets,* II, p. 117.
[107] *Carnets,* I, p. 161.
[108] *MS,* in *Essais,* p. 197.
[109] *Métaphysique Chrétienne,* in *Essais,* p. 1228.
[110] *Carnets,* I, p. 16.
[111] "Le Désert," in *Essais,* pp. 83-84.
[112] *Carnets,* I, p. 117.

is] a reserve of real energy." [113] "Give up the bondage of feminine allurements." [114] "Man's sexual life was given him in order to turn him away from the right path .... Chastity extinguishes the species: therein, perhaps, resides the truth." [115] "Sex is pointless .... Chastity alone can lead to personal progress." [116] "Unchecked sexuality leads to a philosophy of cosmic absurdity; chastity, on the other hand, endows the universe with meaning ...." [117] And this final utterance, worthy of a recluse at Port Royal: "Illness is like a convent: it has its rules, its silences, and its inspirations." [118]

Camus' ascetic ideal, of course, has nothing intrinsically Christian about it. While the only justification of Christian asceticism is (ideally) love, pagan asceticism is a renunciation of pleasure in order to liberate the mind, or to avoid physical or moral pain. Camus' ascetic ideal — in fact he was anything but an ascetic — is far more akin to the ethics of Seneca, Marcus Aurelius, and Lucretius than to the spirituality of Saint Francis. Indeed, some of Camus' more disabusing reflections on sex cannot fail to remind a classicist of those tragic lines of Lucretius, in Book IV: " ... medio de fonte leporum / Surgit amari aliquid, quod in ipsis floribus angat ...." (IV, 1126-27.)

It would be foolish to pretend that Camus had a Christian attitude towards sex. Not only did he never see anything intrinsically immoral about it, he never went so far as to consider sexual morality synonymous with marital fidelity. Voluntary sexual indulgence he termed a "victory," especially when it happens to free one from repressive moral imperatives; [119] and unbridled sexuality he judged rather as (in his own terms) "folly" than as "crime." Chastity did not represent an intrinsic value, was not of itself a "superior" virtue, and was personally meritorious only if it represented a victory of will over instinct. Camus' ascetic tastes, therefore, like those of Don Juan in his declining years, are merely the obverse of his taste for pleasure. The hedonist must learn renunciation, like the athlete, or the saint. [120]

---

[113] *Ibid.,* p. 59.
[114] *Ibid.,* p. 227.
[115] *Carnets,* II, p. 49.
[116] *Ibid.,* p. 51.
[117] *Ibid.,* p. 55.
[118] *Ibid.,* p. 57.
[119] *Ibid.,* p. 51.
[120] *MS,* in *Essais,* p. 151.

It is only fair to remark, however, that Camus felt a strange fascination for the Christian ascetic ideal. His *Notebooks* reveal a curious attraction towards Saint Paul, particularly those letters with anti-feminist passages. He admired what he considered the "heroism" of the vow of celibacy, and once told Jean Grenier that even conjugal fidelity is absurd unless it is sustained by faith in the supernatural. [121] He acknowledged that his particular brand of asceticism could prove "dessicating" for the heart, though it might profit the mind and will. [122] He preferred the Christian asceticism that advises man to mortify himself out of love, to the over-refined self-denials of a Gide, declaring that the former appeared more "natural." [123] He was dispassionate enough, therefore, to understand the spirit in which Christian asceticism is practised, an understanding that few middle-class Christians can claim to share. "Though I do not look upon myself as a Cathar," he once told a journalist, "I have always admired the perfectionist forms of Christianity."

His professed taste for austerity, poverty, and asceticism makes it easier to understand why the word "sanctity" was sometimes annoyingly and erroneously used with reference to the man and artist. Though he was understandably irritated when complacent critics spoke of his goodness, Camus was himself the first to coin the phrase "negative sanctity:"

> How describe that objective, far greater than myself, which I am able to meditate upon and feel, but unable to define? A kind of difficult ascent towards "a sanctity of negation," a heroism without God, in short, pure manhood. A composite of all the human virtues, including isolation from God.
>
> What is it that gives Christianity its superiority *of example,* its only superiority? Christ and his saints — their search for a *style of life.* Each of my works is a step upwards, towards an unrewarded perfection. *The Stranger* is a starting point. *The Myth* also. *The Plague* represents a progression, not from zero to infinity, but towards a deeper complexity that is yet to be defined. The point of arrival will be the

---

[121] Jean Grenier, *Albert Camus,* pp. 138-39.

[122] *Carnets,* II, p. 77.

[123] "L'Eté à Alger," in *Essais,* p. 69 (note): "Le christianisme aussi veut suspendre le désir. Mais, plus naturel [i.e. que Gide], il y voit une mortification."

saint; but he will have an arithmetical value, he will be as measurable as man. [124]

Though Camus' analysis of the soul's progress has something in common with the mystical writings of Spanish mysticism, his conception of the interior life is ultimately far closer in spirit to Marcus Aurelius than to Saint John of the Cross. Yet, without sharing the theocentric Christian idea of sanctity, he showed a deep, dispassionate understanding of it. "Christian sanctity," he writes in his *Notebooks*, "is also a revolt, a refusal of things as they are, an assumption of the misery of the world." [125] In a passage that is astonishingly faithful to the Christian idea of spiritual development, he wrote: "If there is a soul, it is erroneous to believe that it is given to us in its finished state. It is created here, in the course of one's lifetime. Life is nothing other than this long and torturous delivery. Death comes when the soul is ready, fashioned by ourselves and our pains...." [126] Till the last, however, Camus' own conception of sanctity and salvation remained irreducibly anthropocentric. "What he would have liked for all men," Jean Grenier said of him later, "was salvation..., a completely earthly salvation. Camus thought that salvation should be, not the work of a Savior, but of a man who has discovered a 'formula' for lessening man's misery, preaches that formula by example, and finally becomes a saint without faith...." [127]

Never did Camus better comprehend Christianity than when, faithful to its ideal of Incarnation, it "spoke through the body." The dogmatic and juridical features of the Christian religion rarely elicited from him anything other than indifference or hostility. Christianity being, however, the product of a concrete, historical event, its message should be more easily communicable to sense than to intellect. Should it not, therefore, have shared Hellenism's veneration for art? In his responses to this query, Camus ever oscillated between extreme attitudes. There were times when, influenced no doubt by the Gnostic forms of Christianity he knew so well, he interpreted the Christian attitude towards the body in unmistakably dualistic terms. This attitude is particularly noticeable in *Christian Metaphysics*, where he

---

[124] *Carnets*, II, p. 31.
[125] *Ibid.*, p. 298. Camus is in fact paraphrasing Jacques Maritain.
[126] *Carnets*, II, p. 284.
[127] Jean Grenier, *Albert Camus*, p. 144.

interprets Christianity as the culmination of a historical period during which the soul was taking precedence over the body. [128] And there is admittedly but a shade of difference between the pessimism of the early Christians towards the world, and Basilides' contempt for the flesh. Yet, despite historical aberrations, Christianity has usually considered hostility towards the flesh as contrary to its spirit. Saint Paul, for example, never taught that the body was to be destroyed, but that it is the temple of the Spirit, with a capacity for sanctification and glorification. The destruction of Christ's body on the cross is an inseparable event from its resurrection from the tomb. There are moments when Camus understands this point fully: "If this God touches you," he writes of one of Piero della Francesca's "resurrections," "it is because of his human face. Such is the singular limitation of our human condition, that it must endow even those symbols that deny the body with a physical appearance. The symbols succeed in denying the body, but they allow it to retain its prestige. The body is alone generous.... Christianity has understood this. If it has made such an impact, it is through its God made man. The truth and grandeur of this God, however, stops at the cross, at the very moment when he cries out his desolation. Tear out the final pages of the gospel and you are in the presence of a human religion, which suggests a cult of solitude and grandeur...." [129]

"Tear out the final pages of the gospel...." Camus seems to be proposing a Nietzschean Christianity, totally human, immanent, in a word, "Hellenic." The Christianity of the "final pages of the gospel" could never be included, for unlike the preceding pages, they fail to "speak to the body." This point, repeatedly made by Camus — he could not believe in the resurrection of Christ, he said, "because his imagination failed him" — bears closer investigation. The message of the final pages is that Christ rose *bodily* from the tomb, appeared to his disciples, and, finally ascended bodily out of sight. The Greeks, it will be remembered, while believing in the imperishability of the soul, were offended by the idea that the body should ever rise again; yet, whenever Greek mythology, or Greek art, describes the activities of these souls in the netherworld, the souls are necessarily endowed with a body, however ethereal. In brief, any philosophical or artistic

---

[128] *Métaphysique Chrétienne*, in *Essais*, pp. 1227-28.
[129] *Carnets*, I, pp. 205-06.

attempt to describe even the survival of the soul must appeal to the imagination. Camus was perhaps entirely justified in not believing in bodily resurrection; but I fail to see the sense of his attributing his unbelief to a failure of imagination, as, in fact, the resurrection of a body appeals more directly to the senses than the survival of a spirit. It seems curious that, with his knowledge of Giotto, Piero della Francesca, and so many other Florentine treasures of religious art, Camus did not explicitly realize that the Christian idea of physical resurrection after death is entirely *in keeping* with the Christian tendency to give body to abstract truths. The resurrection of Christ from the dead, as well as the final resurrection of mankind, were perhaps the subjects which most impressed the early Christian iconographs, as they did the Renaissance artists.

* * *

Camus was convinced that Christianity is a doctrine of radical injustice; and his conviction seems to have been irreducible. "Christianity in its essence — and therein lies its paradoxical greatness — is a doctrine of injustice, founded upon the sacrifice of an innocent man and the acceptance of this sacrifice. Justice, on the other hand, cannot subsist without rebellion." [130] How often, and in how many different ways, did he voice his concern for replacing love of neighbor by a "simple solicitude for truth, self-effacement, and a taste for human grandeur," as if there existed a necessary choice between charity and truth. [131] Though many of his colleagues and friends offered him proof to the contrary, he seemed incapable of imagining a Christian who does not resign himself to evil. The indifference with which he considered any exceptions to this "law" of Christian resignation somehow made the law itself appear like a fixation. Christianity was in its essence, he thought, a doctrine of injustice. A Christian who rebels is simply stretching the constitutionality of his religion.

On this point, as on so many others, Camus was irreducibly honest; but the very lucidity with which he states the problem does not always preclude ambiguity. Despite his Greek heart, for example, he knew that the ideal of social justice was introduced into the West not by

---

[130] *Actuelles I,* in *Essais,* p. 271.
[131] *Ibid.,* p. 272.

Hellenism, but by Judeo-Christianity. He realized that, on the chapter of justice, the Greek city states were perhaps the last model one should turn to. Certain city states of the fourth century B. C., he noted ruefully, used to swear to counter the interests of the people always. [132] As far as Athenian democracy was concerned, slavery alone had made it possible, as it had provided freemen with the necessary leisure to engage in politics. [133] No, it was history, not nature, that had launched the ideal of justice. Christianity, having invented history, and indirectly given new meaning to the idea of metaphysical rebellion, was at least remotely responsible for placing social justice at the center of man's preoccupations.

Camus would have, and indirectly did, concede this historical point; but, apart from the fact that Christians rarely practise what they preach, the insoluble problem remains a metaphysical one. Camus had an *a priori* conception of the divine omnipotence, which he quite rightly could not reconcile with the existence of evil. The Christian God, theologians say, is all-powerful. If Christ suffered, it is because God wanted him to suffer. If evil "exists" it is because God wishes it to exist. Since God is all powerful, He could change this intolerable situation. If He does not change it, He therefore wants it to be so; and to resign oneself is to accept this state of things.

Camus' syllogisms are a fit rejoinder to all the abstract, "objective" statements that have been made about God through the centuries. In a Camus, the theologian has, as it were, met his match. ("Thou didst not know that I, too, am a logician," says Dante's Lucifer.) To Camus' objections there is no reply, except to remark that the Christian *should* not attempt to invent an abstract structure of "divine attributes," for surely they will end up contradicting one another. The only God the Christian should know is a historical, incarnate God, who, for some reason, decided to share the social condition of the poor and the disinherited, and to take upon himself the misery of this world. The duty of the Christian, then, should be not to make righteous assertions about divine omnipotence, but to revolt against injustice by assuming it. The Christian should revolt against evil by making it his own.

---

[132] *Carnets, I*, p. 251: "Au IVe siècle, dans certaines cités grecques, les oligarches prêtaient ce serment: 'Je serai toujours l'ennemi du peuple et je conseillerai ce que je saurai lui être nuisible.' "

[133] *Ibid.*, pp. 247-48.

There are moments, curiously enough, when Camus felt that Christianity does, at its best, hold to the same ideal he did. Jacques Maritain taught him that Christian sanctity is in fact a refusal to accept the world as it is. [134] Vera Figner had taught him that tyranny and oppression are contrary to the Christian spirit. [135] Virgil Gheorghiu, the Rumanian Orthodox novelist, reminded him that Christ had been executed among thieves. [136] Bernanos had proved to him that a Christian need not necessarily be an admirer of Franco. [137] Somewhere in a primitive past, revolt and indignation had been the mark of the Christian: "He may obstinately choose compromise, or give his condemnations the obscure style of the Papal encyclicals. He may stubbornly allow himself to be robbed of that virtue of revolt and indignation which belonged to him long ago. If that happens, Christianity will die while Christians continue to live.... If Christians set their minds to it, millions of voices, millions, do you hear?, would join with the cry of a handful of isolated men who, without the benefit of faith or law, are now pleading relentlessly all over the world for other men and their children." [138] When he uttered these words to a group of Christians at the Dominican convent of Latour-Maubourg, the Greek heart and the Christian sensibility achieved a perfect, if quite momentary harmony.

* * *

Camus never seriously considered a romantic "return" to Hellenism. He hoped, at best, for a restoration of the equilibrium between nature and history. Yet he never explicitly entertained the possibility that Hellenic and Christian values, if fused together in modern terms, might contain some solutions to the problems he posed. [139] In a sense,

---

[134] *Carnets,* II, p. 298: "La sainteté aussi est une révolte: c'est refuser les choses telles qu'elles sont. C'est prendre sur soi le malheur du monde."

[135] *Ibid.,* p. 231.

[136] *Ibid.,* p. 275.

[137] "Pourquoi l'Espagne?," *Actuelles I,* in *Essais,* p. 394. To Gabriel Marcel, who could not understand Camus' objections to the Franquist regime, Camus replied: "Bernanos n'aurait pas écrit ce que vous avez écrit sur ce sujet."

[138] "L'Incroyant et les Chrétiens," *Actuelles I,* in *Essais,* p. 375.

[139] Camus was opposed to the romantic idea of returning to a Medieval or even Hellenic past, "as if we had learned nothing in the meantime." (*Carnets,* II, p. 26).

and without any irony intended, Christianity provided a solution far too accessible to satisfy Camus' unquestionable taste for impossible ideals. Considered in a more favorable light, Christianity might have provided him with hope for a resurrection of ancient values, even those Hellenic values he so prized. But even hope is a sign of weakness, perhaps the last and worst of mankind's ills. Camus once cited the myth of Pandora as evidence that the Greeks had always refused to hope. On this point, as on so many others, he had read the Greeks with haste. His pessimism, in fact, has nothing Greek about it. His overemphasis on absurdity (a versatile, but hardly viable intellectual concept), his vision of a natural order completely cut off from the world of gods and heroes can only lead, in the final analysis, to an impoverishment of the natural order itself. His universe is singularly devoid of the variety, the joy, and the plenitude that characterize the world of Pindar, Aeschylus, Sophocles, and Plato. There was no part of life the Greeks ever refused, not even hope. Camus' heroes are different. They avidly inhale a few passing joys, teeter, then disappear from a world wherein they were strangers from the first. A flash, a spark, nothing more. Nothing ties them to the cosmos, nothing links their personal destiny to the living universe that surrounds them. [140]

If it be a Christian disease to feel dispossessed and cast adrift in a hostile universe, it is fair to say that, although Camus fought that disease tooth and nail, he never entirely convalesced. I am rather inclined to think, however, that his metaphysical malaise was more Gnostic than Christian, the product, as it were, of a Graeco-Christian germ. That matter is reserved for the following chapter.

---

[140] Cf. A. Roynet, "Albert Camus chez les Chrétiens," in *La Vie Intellectuelle* (April, 1949), pp. 348-49.

CHAPTER III

GNOSTIC SOLUTIONS: *CALIGULA*

The second chapter of the essay on Christian Metaphysics is devoted to an exploration of Gnosticism during the second and third centuries of the Christian era. In a brief introduction Camus describes the movement as "one of the first experiments in Graeco-Christian collaboration," as "a Greek meditation on Christian themes," and as "a metaphysical kermess erected upon Christian foundations." [1] Christ's Incarnation and Redemption, he continues, are common themes in all the writings of the Christian Gnostics, but Christ is but one of a plethora of "mediators" between the human order and the divine. While it is possible to speak of several "generations" of Christian Gnosticism over a period of two centuries, the general movement can be defined as "a philosophical and religious teaching dispersed to a group of initiates, based upon a mixture of Christian dogmas and pagan philosophy, and assimilating the exotic and brilliant elements of the most diverse religions." [2]

Gnosticism, Camus suggests, posed its metaphysical problems in Christian terms and resolved them with Greek formulas. Basilides and Marcion, both Gnostics of the "first generation," were convinced of the ugliness and evil of this world and of the abyss that separates it from God, an abyss so great that only a superior knowledge of God (*gnōsis*) is capable of bridging this infinite cleavage and saving man from annihilation. The Gnostics' conviction that man and the

---

[1] A. Camus, *Métaphysique Chrétienne et Néoplatonisme*, in *Essais*, pp. 1250-52.

[2] *Ibid.*, p. 1251.

world are as nothing and that man can be saved only by being united with the divine was their particular way of formulating the themes of Incarnation and Redemption. In their view, however, the Incarnation and the Redemption were meant for a small elite. Valentinus, for example, divides humanity into three orders: the "hylics" (or "materials"), the "psychics," and the "spirituals." Only the latter live in God and know Him; but theirs is a knowledge that can be transmitted to others. Salvation, in short, is a teachable reality. [3]

In section one of the chapter, entitled "The Gnostic Solution and its Themes," Camus summarizes the main tenets of Basilides, Marcion, and Valentinus, as well as those of lesser-known Gnostic sects, such as the Naassenes, the Perates, and the Sethians. [4] The four fundamental Gnostic "themes," he concludes, are: the problem of evil, the duality of Gods (superior and inferior), the theory of intermediaries, and the incommunicability of the "superior" God.

The problem of evil is at the core of all Gnostic thinking, particularly that of Basilides. This Christian thinker, who lived during the reigns of Hadrian and Antoninus Pius, was particularly obsessed with the problem of sin and its causes. Convinced that man was naturally predisposed to sin, Basilides taught that sin invariably entails its own punishment; and conversely, that whoever suffers must necessarily have sinned, lest God be otherwise open to the accusation of inflicting gratuitous suffering upon mankind. The Christian martyrs, therfore, as well as Christ himself, were guilty of sin. Suffering is always a means of achieving repentance and redemption. [5]

Marcion (whose ideas Tertullian publicized and refuted in his *Adversus Marcionem*) held that there were two divinities: a superior God of the invisible world, and an inferior God of the visible world. The superior God did not reveal himself through his Creation, but through Jesus Christ. The other God, "cruel and warlike," is the God of the Old Testament, Creator of the material world. St. Paul's antitheses between "Law and Gospel," "Flesh and Spirit," "Judaïsm and Christianity," offer scriptural evidence, according to Marcion, that the Yahweh of the Old Testament and the "Father" of the New are locked in an eternal struggle. Christ is the emissary sent by the

---

[3] *Ibid.*, p. 1252.

[4] *Ibid.*, pp. 1252-64.

[5] *Ibid.*, pp. 1252-55.

"superior" God to wrest the created world from the hands of this cruel, bellicose adversary. Marcion's moral precepts are a logical consequence of his metaphysics. He recommends sexual abstinence as a means of defying the Old Testament God's enjoinder to "increase and multiply." Marcion's asceticism, in short, is a form of metaphysical rebellion: "The style of life proposed by Marcion is an ascetic one, but it is an asceticism of pride. One must despise the things of this world out of hatred for the Creator. His domination must be given as little a hold as possible. Such is Marcion's ideal. His asceticism is, consequently, of the extremest sort. If he preaches sexual abstinence, it is only because the God of the Old Testament has said: "Increase and multiply." This pessimistic view of the world and this arrogant refusal to submit have an entirely modern resonance about them. Taking the problem of evil as his point of departure, [Marcion] considers the world as evil, but refuses to believe that God can be its author." 6

Valentinus, a Gnostic of the "second generation," was especially known for his original theory of intermediaries. Whereas the Gnostics of the first generation considered God as ineffable and incommunicable, Valentinus viewed Creation as a "metaphysical kermess." His eonology is a bizarre mixture of Christian and Greek mythology. In the beginning, writes Valentinus, God was both solitary and perfect. In a display of superabundance, He created the original dyad of Spirit and Truth. They, in turn, engendered the Word and Life, which produced Man and the Church. From these six original principles sprang a plethora of angels and eons, one called "Decade," the other "Dodecade." 7

According to Valentinus, humanity is divided into three categories according to the extent to which they are conscious of their origins: the spirituals, whose only desire is for God; the hylics, who neither know nor wish to know where they come from; and, between them, the psychics, who alternate between gross sensuality and unresolved metaphysical anxiety. 8 Man was redeemed not by Jesus, but by the Spirit; God is not the author of evil; only the "Gnostics" (or "spirituals"), that is, those who assume consciousness of where they come

---

6 *Ibid.*, pp. 1255-57.
7 *Ibid.*, p. 1259.
8 *Ibid.*, p. 1260.

from, can be saved; salvation is contemporaneous with knowledge: such are the main tenets of Valentinus' complex system. [9]

Gnosticism, concludes Camus, was a hybrid product spawned by the encounter of Hellenism with Christianity, and by their inability to merge entirely with each other. A number of Gnostic themes were a product of the Platonic tradition, such as the emanation of divinities from the Godhead, the anxiety of the human spirit while it is trapped in matter, and the regeneration of the soul when it returns to its original source. Gnosticism borrowed from Christianity its dogma of the Incarnation but transformed it beyond recognition. Christian also was the Gnostics' obsession with evil and their belief in the drama of history. [10]

Stretching well ower two centuries, Camus concludes, Gnosticism was an amalgamation of the various religious and philosophical systems abroad in the Mediterranean during the Hellenistic age. Gnosticism fashioned a monstrous Christianity, spiced with some ingredients of Oriental religion and Greek thought: it was Christian in its obsession with the problem of evil, Christian in its conception of God's omnipotence and man's nothingness, Greek in its conviction that *gnōsis* is the way to salvation. Historically, it showed Christianity "the road it should not follow," and demonstrated some of the more eccentric combinations made possible by the encounter of Hellenism and Christianity. [11]

Camus' summary of the various forms of Gnostic thought, however prolix, fragmentary, and (occasionally) confusing, was a faithful recapitulation of two main sources: Eugène de Faye's *Gnostiques et Gnosticisme*, [12] and E. Amelineau's *Essai sur le Gnosticisme Egyptien*. [13] Gnosticism being a particularly recondite subject, it is understandable that chapter two of *Christian Metaphysics* should be the most "academic," the least personal of Camus' essay. There are, as usual, some remarkable similarities of phrasing that attest to Camus' dependence on his scholarly sources:

---

[9] *Ibid.*, pp. 1260-61.
[10] *Ibid.*, pp. 1265-66.
[11] *Ibid.*, pp. 1268-69.
[12] E. de Faye, *Gnostiques et Gnosticisme*, Paris, 1913.
[13] A. Amelineau, *Essai sur le Gnosticisme Egyptien*, Paris, 1887.

A. Camus, *Métaphysique Chrétienne,* in *Essais,* Paris, 1965.

E. de Faye, *Gnostiques et Gnosticisme,* Paris, 1913.

"*L'origine et la cause de cette mauvaise doctrine, dit Epiphane, c'est la recherche et la discussion du problème du Mal.*" [Footnote 2: *Contr. Haer,* XXIV, 6 72c.] C'est en effet ce qui ressort du peu que l'on sait de la pensée basilidienne. Eloigné de toute spéculation, il ne s'attache qu'au problème moral, et plus précisement à ce problème moral qui naît des rapports de l'homme et de Dieu." (p. 1253.)

"... il est permis de conclure que les préoccupations toutes morales que nous révèlent les fragments étaient au premier plan de la pensée de [Basilide]. Au surplus, c'est ce qu'Epiphane lui-même donne à entendre. *L'origine et la cause, dit-il, de cette mauvaise doctrine, c'est la recherche et la discussion du problème du mal.* [Note: *Epiph: Contra Haereses,* XXIV, 6, 72c.] (p. 51.)

"Marcien n'est pas un spéculatif mais un génie religieux." (p. 1255.)

"C'est un esprit religieux, nullement spéculatif." (p. 143.)

"D'une façon générale sa pensée tourne autour de trois points: 1e Dieu; 2e la Rédemption et la personne du Christ; 3e la Morale." (p. 1255.)

"Doctrine de Dieu, doctrine de la rédemption, doctrine de la personne de Jésus - Christ, morale, voilà les points sur lesquels ont porté les réflexions de Marcion." (p. 152.)

"Il y a deux divinités pour Marcion: l'une, *supérieure,* règne dans le monde invisible, l'autre, *subalterne,* est le Dieu de ce monde." (p. 1255.)

"D'après lui, il y a deux divinités, l'une *supérieure,* l'autre *subalterne.*" (pp. 152-3.)

"C'est que le deuxième Dieu, *juge cruel et belliqueux,* est le dieu de l'Ancien Testament..." (p. 1256.)

"Nous savons [dit Tertullien] que Marcion affirme l'existence de deux dieux différents; le second est un *juge, cruel et belliqueux ...*" (pp. 153-4.)

"Emancipateur autant que Rédempteur, il est *l'organe d'une sorte de coup d'Etat métaphysique ...*" (p. 1256.)

"Délivrance de quoi? De la domination du créateur ... *L'organe de cette révolution,* c'est *Jésus-Christ.*" (p. 163.)

"*C'est par haine du Créateur* qu'il faut mépriser les biens de ce monde ..." (p. 1257.)

"*C'est par haine du Créateur* que Marcion pratique la continence ..." (p. 169.)

Camus' chapter on Gnosticism was a fertile sourcebook for the preparation of at least two of his later works. His reference to the Homeric *Hymn to Demeter* and to the Eleusinian mysteries, in *Noces à Tipasa,* is taken literally from chapter two of *Christian Metaphysics*:

Métaphysique Chrétienne, in *Essais,* Paris, 1965.	"Noces à Tipasa," in *Essais,* Paris, 1965.
"L'initiation donne prise à l'homme sur le royaume divin. Le salut l'y introduit sans qu'il ait aucune part à ce succès. On peut croire à Dieu sans pour cela être sauvé. *Aux mystères d'Eleusis il suffisait de contempler.* [Note 1: Hymne homérique à Déméter, 480-483 "*Heureux, celui des hommes vivant sur la terre qui a vu ces choses.* Mais celui qui n'a pas été initié aux cérémonies sacrées et celui qui y a pris part n'auront jamais la même destinée après la mort dans les vastes ténèbres." (p. 1252.)	"Est-il même à Déméter ce vieil hymne à qui plus tard je songerai sans contrainte: *Heureux celui des vivants sur la terre qui a vu ces choses.*' Voir, et voir sur cette terre, comment oublier la leçon? *Aux mystères d'Eleusis, il suffisait de contempler.* (p. 67.)

In *The Rebel,* Camus' analysis of the Gnostic effort to "promote" the concept of an "accessible" God (in contrast to the authoritarian God of Judaïsm), is in fact a brief summary of the second chapter of *Christian Metaphysics*:

> Gnosticism, which is the fruit of Greco-Christian collaboration, has tried for two centuries, in reaction against Judaic thought, to promote this concept [i.e. the concept of a God accessible to man]. We know, for example, the vast number of intercessors invented by Valentinus. But the eons of this particular metaphysical skirmish are the equivalent of the intermediary truths to be found in Hellenism. Their aim is to diminish the absurdity of an intimate relationship between suffering humanity and an implacable god. This is the special role of Marcion's cruel and bellicose second god. This demiurge is responsible for the creation of a finite world and of death. Our duty is to hate him and at the same time to deny everything that he has created, by means of asceticism, to the point of destroying, by sexual abstinence, all creation.

This form of asceticism is therefore both proud and rebellious. Marcion simply alters the course of rebellion and directs it toward an inferior god so as to be better able to exalt the superior god. Gnosis, owing to its Greek origins, remains conciliatory and tends to destroy the Judaic heritage in Christianity. [14]

A confrontation of this text, in its original version, with some of Camus' assertions in chapter two of *Christian Metaphysics*, provides interesting correspondences:

Métaphysique Chrétienne, in *Essais*, 1965.	*L'Homme Révolté*, in *Essais*, Paris, 1965.
"... on doit considérer l'hérésie gnostique *comme un des premiers essais de collaboration gréco-chrétienne*." (p. 1250.)	"Le gnosticisme, qui est *le fruit d'une collaboration gréco-chrétienne*, a tenté pendant deux siècles, en réaction contre la pensée judaïque, d'accenteur ce mouvement." (p. 444.)
"Et sur les quelques aspirations simples et passionnées du Christianisme, ils bâtissent... *tout un décor de kermesse métaphysique*." (p. 1250.)	"Mais les éons *de cette kermesse métaphysique* jouent le même rôle que les v é r i t é s intermédiaires dans l'hellénisme." (p. 444.)
"C'est que le *deuxième Dieu, juge cruel et belliqueux* [de Marcion] est le dieu de l'Ancien Testament..." (p. 1256.)	"C'est le rôle [i.e. le mal] du *deuxième dieu cruel et belliqueux de Marcion*." (p. 444.)
"La régle de vie que propose Marcion est ascétique. Mais c'est un ascétisme d'orgueil. C'est par haine du Créateur qu'il faut mépriser les biens de ce monde: donnez le moins de prise à sa domination c'est l'idéal de Marcion.... Et si Marcion prêche l'abstinence sexuelle c'est parce que le Dieu de l'Ancien Testament a dit: "Croissez et multipliez." (p. 1257.)	"Nous devons le hair [i.e. le Dieu cruel] en même temps que nous devons nier sa création, par l'ascèse jusqu'à la détruire grâce à l'abstinence sexuelle. Il s'agit donc d'une ascèse orgueilleuse et révoltée" (p. 444.)

---

[14] A. Camus, *The Rebel*, trans. by A. Bower (New York, 1967), pp. 32-33.

"Selon lui [Basilide]..., il faut... conclure que les martyrs ont péché... Le Christ n'échappe pas à la loi universelle du peché." (p. 1254.)

"Pour Basilide, par exemple, les martyrs ont péché, et le Christ lui-même, puisqu'ils souffrent." (p. 444.)

More difficult to discern, but equally relevant to the present subject, is the presence in Camus' writings of what might be described as a "Gnostic residue." Camus never explicitly denied what Marcel Moré once called his "sympathy for the perfectionist forms of Christianity: Gnostics, Cathars, Jansenists." [15] Like Basilides and Valentinus (and Augustine, during his Manichean period), Camus seems to have considered evil as an ontological "substance." His concepts of absurdity, alienation and tragic revolt, as Simone Petrement has pointed out, are current versions of ancient Gnostic ideas. [16] Like the Gnostics, Camus felt that reality perpetually contradicts itself; his thinking is impregnated with a Manichean dualism, which transpires in his abundant use of antitheses ("l'envers et l'endroit," "le oui et le non," "l'ombre et la lumière," "la nature et l'histoire," "cette vie et l'autre vie"). His vision of historical and modern Christianity invariably tended toward Gnostic deviations. Like Simone Weil (and Marcion), he felt that God must be considered absolutely innocent if suffering is not to be imputed to Him. [17] The author of the *Myth of Sisyphus*, "a stranger to himself and to the world," "armed only with a *gnosis* which denies itself the moment it is asserted," feels that he "*must* choose between contemplation and action, this world and the next." The latter choice recalls Valentinus' sharp division of humanity between "hylics" and "spirituals," and the undecided "psychics" in between. [18] In *The Rebel*, very much like Marcion, Camus speaks of

---

[15] A. Camus, *Actuelles II*, in *Essais*, p. 745.

[16] S. Petrement, "La Gnose en Notre Temps," in *Encyclopédie Française*, vol. XIX, *Philosophie, Religion* (Paris, 1957), section 19-34-10 sq.

[17] A. Camus, *Carnets*, II, p. 271: "Dieu doit être absolument innocent."

[18] A. Camus, *Le Mythe de Sisyphe*, in *Essais*, p. 112: "Etranger à moi-même et à ce monde, armé pour tout secours d'une pensée qui se nie elle-même dès qu'elle s'affirme, quelle est cette condition où je ne puis avoir la paix....?" Cf. *Ibid.*, p. 165: "Il vient toujours un temps où il faut choisir entre la contemplation et l'action.... Il faut vivre avec le temps et mourir avec lui ou s'y soustraire pour une plus grande vie." In the same essay (p. 189), Camus declares that "the history of the Gnostic audacities and the persistence of Manichean doctrines did more for the construction of orthodox dogma than any combination of prayers."

Christ as a *mediator* whose essential function it was to "diminish the absurdity of a head-on confrontation between a miserable humanity and an implacable God." [19] In a sharply-worded reply to François Mauriac, Camus referred to Christ's death (in Valentinian and Jansenist terms), as having been meant "for a few, but not for us." [20] And in *Exile and the Kingdom,* the renegade missionary, having been subjected to the most savage brutality, abjures the Christian God in order to worship an evil Fetish not unlike Marcion's "cruel and bellicose judge." The missionary's monologue is a veritable Gnostic hymn: "Hail! he was the master, the only lord, whose indisputable attribute was malice, there are no good masters . . . . I surrendered to him and approved his maleficent order, I adored in him the evil principle of this world . . . . I had been misled, solely the reign of malice was devoid of defects, I had been misled . . . good is an idle dream . . . its reign is impossible. Only evil can reach its limits and reign absolutely, it must be served to establish its visible kingdom . . . only evil is present, down with Europe, reason, honor, and the cross. . . . Yes, the Fetish alone has power, he is the sole god of this world, hatred is his commandment . . . and I swore to him to save my new faith, my true master, my despotic God . . . ." [21]

* * *

Camus' interest in Gnosticism, and in the rapport of modern nihilism with Gnosticism, was perhaps nowhere more evident than in *Caligula.* It would be exaggerated to describe the play merely as an attempt to dramatize what Camus' called "the Gnostic solution," yet if (as I am convinced), many of Camus' plays illustrate not merely his lasting obsession with moral and metaphysical evil, but his attempt to dramatize certain "solutions," *Caligula* would seem to be an experimentation with the "Gnostic solution." [22] Caligula's dissatisfaction

[19] A. Camus, *L'Homme Révolté,* in *Essais,* p. 444.

[20] A. Camus, *Actuelles I,* in *Essais,* p. 287: "je crois avoir une idée juste de la grandeur du Christianisme, mais nous sommes quelques-uns dans ce monde persécuté à avoir le sentiment que si le Christ est mort pour certains, il n'est pas mort pour nous . . . ."

[21] A. Camus, "The Renegade," in *Exile and the Kingdom,* trans. by Justin O'Brien (New York, 1963), pp. 53-57.

[22] The word "solutions" occurs frequently in *Christian Metaphysics.* Every philosophical and religious movement from Epicurus to Saint Augustine rep-

with a physical universe that he considers evil; his dualistic obsession with the concepts of purity and impurity; his faith in a superior knowledge, of which he is the purveyor, as the sole means of escaping from the realm of the possible; his contemptuous asceticism in matters of love and friendship, or anything that implies an admission of value; his radical conviction that all men are guilty; his sense of history, that is, his vision of life as a drama, as an inescapable engagement in a process toward catastrophe — these ideas bear a close resemblance to those which Camus in *Christian Metaphysics* had called "the fundamental Gnostic themes."

Caligula, of course, is not a Gnostic in strict, doctrinal terms. Indeed, one of the major tenets of all Gnostic thinking, as Camus realized, was the existence of a supreme God of the invisible world, whose nature is alien to the universe. In *Caligula,* the Gnostic God is "replaced" by the idea of *l'impossible.* What is fundamentally Gnostic about this abstract divinity, however, is that it can only be designated negatively (the Gnostics, too, conceive the transcendent God in negative terms). [23] Caligula's *impossible,* like the Gnostic God, is unknowable to the ordinary mind but accessible to an initiated few means of an illumination (*gnōsis*), which Caligula calls "connaissance." [24] The initiation of the elect requires a negation of all cosmic values, expressed either by an ascetic contempt for the things of the world, or by an indiferent overindulgence in them. Caligula's vision, like the Gnostic vision, is fundamentally *acosmic,* alien to the world of the possible. So long as they remain prisoners of the cosmos "men die and they are not happy." Consequently, though Caligula's *impossible* is a different conception from the supreme divinity of the Gnostic system, his view of the world, the structures of his thinking, and his

---

resents, in Camus' view, an attempt to "resolve" the problem of moral and natural evil.

[23] A. Camus, *Métaphysique Chrétienne . . . ,* in *Essais,* p. 1258: "La première génération gnostique se contentait de considérer Dieu comme ineffable et inexprimable . . . Les successeurs allèrent encore plus loin et certaines de leurs expressions font souvent penser au Brahman des "Upanishads," qui ne peut se définir que par: 'non, non.' " Cf. Robert M. Grant, *Gnosticism* (New York, 1961), p. 16: ". . . the supremely transcendent God . . . is essentially *unknown* and *unknowable . . . .* Between the world and God, therefore, the Gnostics postulated the existence of spiritual beings with a history of their own."

[24] A. Camus, *Caligula,* I, iv, in *Théâtre, Récits, Nouvelles* (Gallimard, 1962), p. 16.

fundamental moral options and projects are Gnostic. It is, in any case, the purpose of this section to demonstrate the plausibility of such a suggestion.

As the play begins Caligula has just returned from a self-imposed exile of three days. His first dialogue with Helicon makes it clear that the significance of his absence has been entirely metaphysical. Caligula has crossed a philosophical wilderness, and upon returning he discovers that his metaphysics is entirely transformed. No longer will he heed the Hellenic admonition to confine himself to the realm of the possible. He has cast aside a cosmic world-view in favor of its perverted, acosmic counterpart. Rather than confine himself to the possible, he will seek after something insane or impossible: immortality, happiness, non-being. He will forsake the solar world for the lunar world. The moon becomes a projection of Caligula's *gnōsis,* a symbol of his desire for an impossible, pure, supra-mundane world, free of the evil gods. It is significant that Caligula's dissatisfaction with this world and his consequent need for the moon are expressed in epistemological terms. In the opening dialogue between Caligula and Helicon, the emperor twice uses the verb *savoir*:

CALIGULA

... I suddenly felt a desire for the impossible ... Things as they are, in my opinion, are far from satisfactory.

HELICON

Many people share your opinion.

CALIGULA

That is so. But in the past I didn't realize it [je ne le *savais* pas]. Now I know [je *sais*]. ... I want ... something ... which isn't of this world. [25]

As the dialogue continues, the use of epistemological language be-'comes more and more varied:

---

[25] A. Camus, *Caligula and Cross Purpose,* trans. by Stuart Gilbert (New Directions, 1947), pp. 13-14. All subsequent references to *Caligula* are taken from this translation. Act and page references will be placed immediately after each quotation.

HELICON

That's sound enough in *theory*. Only in practice one can't
carry it through to its conclusion.

CALIGULA

... You're wrong there. It's just because no one dares to
follow up his *ideas* to the end that nothing is achieved. All
that's needed, I should say, is to be *logical* right through,
at all costs.... I can *see*, too, what you're *thinking* ... I
swear to you her [Drusilla's] death is not the point; it's no
more than the *symbol* of a truth that makes the moon essential to me. A childishly simple, obvious, almost silly
truth ....

HELICON

May I know what it is, this *truth* that you've discovered?

CALIGULA

... Men die; and they are not happy.

HELICON

... Anyhow, Caligula, it's a *truth* with which one comes to
terms, without much trouble. Only look at the people over
there. This *truth* of yours doesn't prevent them from enjoying
their meal.

CALIGULA

... All it proves is that I'm surrounded by *lies* and *self-
deception*. But I've had enough of that; I wish men to live
by the light of *truth*. ... They're without *understanding* and
they need a *teacher*; someone who *knows* what he's talking
about. (I, pp. 14-15.)

That Caligula is highly intelligent and fond of abstract talk does
not in itself satisfactorily explain the epistemological orientation of
his speech to Helicon. After three days of intensive soul-searching he
has visibly experienced an initial illumination. In Gnostic terms,
he has passed from the "physical" and "psychic" levels of consciousness to the "spiritual" level. [26] His negative revelation that men die

---

[26] Camus describes the Gnostic categorization of humanity in the following terms (*Métaphysique Chrétienne ...*, p. 1260): "Ces hommes se di-

and are not happy (i.e., that this world is evil and unacceptable), is counterpoised by the positive revelation that the only "solution" consists of a "connaissance supérieure," which he, as initiating mentor, will impart to his followers.

The first dialogue with Helicon brings to light three major Gnostic themes: than man feels alienated in the universe ("les choses, telles qu'elles sont, ne me semblent pas satisfaisantes"); that there exists an invisible world, transcending ordinary knowledge, which Caligula designates metaphorically as "la lune," and conceptually as "l'impossible;" [27] that the ascent from the evil world of possibility to the pure, lunar realm of impossibility cannot be achieved without a superior knowledge and a contemptuous rejection of all that is traditionally considered as ontologically valuable. Before Caligula's illumination, love and death were valuable in themselves; but from a Gnostic perspective they are the mere signs of a new truth, that all that is "cosmic" is of no value.

As Act I progresses, it becomes clear that Caligula's conversion is irrevocable and that the uninitiated minds about him have begun to notice the difference in his conduct. Before Drusilla's death (and his consequent illumination), Caligula was hedonistic in his morals and Platonistic in his ontology. Although he did not consider the cosmos with absolute seriousness, he did look upon it as a means of access to "ideal" values such as love, friendship, power, intellect, and pleasure. It is of that "other" Caligula, the idealist, that Helicon says, most perceptively: "My dear Caesonia, Caius is an idealist as we all know. Which is another way of saying that he hasn't yet understood. . . . But if he begins to understand, he is capable . . . of taking

---

visent en trois catégories suivant le degré de conscience qu'ils ont de leur origine. . . . Mais ils portent tous la marque de leur naissance: ils ont été faits de crainte, d'*ignorance* et de douleur. D'où la nécessité d'une rédemption." For Caligula, redemption from the torpor and ugliness of this life comes essentially through the channel of *knowledge*.

[27] Caligula's quasi-sexual love of the moon is a detail that Camus borrowed from Suetonius (*Caligula*, XXII, in *Suétone, Vies des Douze Césars,* ed. by H. Aillond, Paris, 1932, p. 78): "Et noctibus quidem plenam fulgentemque lunam invitabat assidue in amplexus atque concubitum . . . ." Although Suetonius narrates this detail as one of many signs of Caligula's madness, a fascination with astral phenomena is also a characteristically Gnostic fixation (see Robert M. Grant, *op. cit.,* p. 17).

charge of everything." [28] Helicon realizes that Caligula has begun to "understand," and that the metaphysical consequence of this understanding will be "de s'occuper de tout," i.e. to negate the cosmos *in its entirety,* rather than pay lip service to its relative value. The old Caligula was a Platonic dualist who considered the cosmos, if not identical with true Being, yet as a stepping stone, a means of access to it. The "new" Caligula is a radical dualist who "sees nothing but his own idea." Having mentally destroyed a cosmos that he finds void of ontological value, he concentrates on his idea, which one might liken to the Gnostic pneuma. [29]

When Caligula sets about "disrupting the political economy" of the Empire, his listeners do not seem to apprehend the metaphysical implications of his "new" message on the state of the Empire: "... We are extremely interested in our Treasury. Everything's important: our fiscal system, public morals, foreign policy, army equipment and agrarian laws. Everything's of cardinal importance, I assure you. And everything's on an equal footing: the grandeur of Rome and your attacks of arthritis...." (I, p. 18.) Caesonia has just finished telling Caligula that she considers matters of public finance secondary (in relation to her body, which her former lover, consistent with his Gnostic world-view, has begun to despise). [30] Caesonia is hoping she can make him come out of his crisis of irrational asceticism which,

---

[28] Act I, 5, my translation. Gilbert's translation of this passage is an inadequate abbreviation. It fails to convey the important point that Caligula's conversion is the product of a transformed *understanding.*

[29] Hans Jonas, *The Gnostic Religion* (Boston, 1958), pp. 268-69: "[For the Gnostics] the world and one's belonging to it are not to be taken seriously. But virtue *is* seriousness in the execution of the different modes of this belonging and the taking seriously of oneself in meeting the demands of the world, i.e. of being. *If as in Platonism the world is not identical with true being, it is yet a stepping stone to it. But 'this world' of gnostic dualism is not even that.* And as a dimension of existence it does not offer occasion to the perfectibility of man. The least, then, that the acosmic attitude must cause in the relation to inner worldly existence is the mental reservation of 'as though not'."

[30] Caligula's "ascetic" attitude towards his mistress during the play is a conscious expression of contempt for all that is traditionally considered as humanly and ontologically valuable. That Caligula should indulge in occasional moments of lechery is in keeping with his neo-Gnostic view of the universe. The laws "thou shalt," "thou shalt not" are just another form of the tyranny of the conventional gods. Caligula, as "professor" of a higher science can afford to be ascetic or libertine, beyond good and evil.

she assumes, is merely one of his many fancies: "The only god I've ever had is my body," she declares, "and now I shall pray this god of mine to give Caius back to me." (I, p. 17.) Caligula's reply means, in substance, that if the entire physical universe is devoid of value, then everything is "important," and on the same ontological footing, whether it be Caesonia's arthritis or the grandeur of Rome.

After telling his Intendant of a plan to fatten the public Treasury by executing an established list of Patricians, Caligula provides Scipio, Cherea, and Caesonia with a lucid account of his "new logic." "I have resolved to be logical," he tells the Intendant, "and . . . presently you'll see what logic's going to cost you." (I, p. 20.) Horrified by Caligula's new vision of Empire, Scipio counters with the Hellenic argument that any game without limits is "a lunatic's pastime." (I, p. 20.) Caligula's reply is consistent with his acosmic vision of reality: to accept limits of any sort implies that the stuff of the world has a prior intelligent structure. From a Gnostic perspective, the sole value is the boundless, unfettered freedom of the spirit: ". . . Ah, my dears, at last I've come to see the uses of supremacy. It gives impossibilities a run. From this day on, so long as life is mine, my freedom has no frontier." (I, p. 21.)

Caligula later gives Cherea a variant version of this same message. The conversation centers about Caligula's hatred of *littérateurs*. Caligula's reasons for abhorring men of letters and poets, and the sneering tones with which he expresses his contempt, are characteristically Gnostic. [31] Poets are liars, and their biggest lie is to bestow value upon people and things. Plato, it will be remembered, mistrusted poets because, by painting the world of appearances in attractive colors, they seduced their readers into mistaking appearance for Reality. Caligula's fundamental reason for hating poets is more radical yet: they deceive us by pretending that Reality has any importance (i.e., that essence exists at all). [32]

---

[31] In this respect, again, he is different from Suetonius' Caligula, who hated men of letters for petty, egotistical reasons, as he hated all great men, present and past. The historical Caligula had thought of destroying Homer's poems, not for the same reasons as Plato, but simply to prove that if Plato could do it, so could he! (Suétone, *Caligula, op. cit.*)

[32] The radical dualism of the Gnostics explains why both the Neo-platonists and the Christian Fathers were hostile to their doctrines. Plotinus (in *Enneads*, II, 9) considered the Gnostics as blasphemous detractors of the world. Irenaeus (*Adversus Haereses*, II 3, 2) considered the Gnostic attitude

CALIGULA

... I don't like literary men, and I can't bear lies.

CHEREA

If we lie, it's often without knowing it. I plead Not Guilty.

CALIGULA

Lies are never guiltless. And yours attribute importance to people and to things. That's what I cannot forgive you.

CHEREA

And yet — since this world is the only one we have, why not plead its cause?

CALIGULA

Your pleading comes too late, the verdict's given. ... This world has no importance; once a man realizes that, he wins his freedom .... And that is why I hate you, you and your kind; because you are not free. You see in me the one free man in the whole Roman Empire. You should be glad to have at last among you an emperor who points the way to freedom. (I, pp. 21-2)

The Gnostic themes of cosmic evil, of liberation through knowledge, and of the need for an initiating teacher occur again in this dialogue. Implicit in the dialogue are the dualistic antitheses between matter and *pneuma*, cosmic imprisonment and Gnostic "freedom," poetic lying and superior knowledge.

In the final scene of Act I, Caligula's Gnostic ideas clash radically with his mistress's Hellenic world-view. Caesonia's attitude is fundamentally cosmic, rational, and esthetic. The order of the world is as it is; any talk of changing it is hubristic, for it is an attempt to be like the gods. Caligula's attitude is acosmic and voluntaristic: the cosmos contains no inherent order, or it is a creation of evil gods. It must therefore be destroyed. To his Gnostic faith in the value of knowledge, *ascesis,* and will, Caligula joins a modernist worship of action and power. He is a Marcion who sounds occasionally like Zarathustra:

---

towars the world "as a product of fall and ignorance," and as "the greatest blasphemy." (Cf. Hans Jonas, *op. cit.,* pp. 253-54.)

CALIGULA

... What's the use to me of a firm hand, what use is the amazing power that's mine, if I can't have the sun set in the east, if I can't reduce the sum of suffering and make an end of death? No, Caesonia, it's all one whether I sleep or keep awake, if I've no power to tamper with the scheme of things.

CAESONIA

But that's madness, sheer madness. It's wanting to be a god on earth.

CALIGULA

So you, too, think I'm mad. And yet — what is a god that I should wish to be his equal? No, it's something higher, far above the gods that I'm aiming at, longing for with all my heart and soul. I am taking over a kingdom where the impossible is king.

CAESONIA

You cannot prevent the sky from being the sky, or a fresh young face from ageing, or a man's heart from growing cold.

CALIGULA

... I want to drown the sky in the sea, to infuse ugliness with beauty, to wring a laugh from pain.

CAESONIA

... There's good and bad, high and low, justice and injustice. And I swear to you these will never change. [33]

CALIGULA

... And I'm resolved to change them.

Pessimistic as to the condition of the lower world, Caligula is confident of the ultimate victory of the "kingdom above the gods" over

---

[33] Caesonia's replies to Caligula are a vibrant echo of the following text of Plato's *Timaeus* (30, B; 34A): 'the universe was considered to be the perfect exemplar of order, and at the same time the cause of all order in particulars, which only in degrees can approximate that of the whole. Again, since the sensible aspect of order is beauty, its inner principle reason, the All as perfect order must be both beautiful and rational in the highest degree." (Cf. H. Jonas, *op. cit.*, p. 242.)

the inferior world of the possible: "And when all is levelled out, when the impossible has come to earth and the moon is in my hands — then, perhaps, I shall be transfigured and the world renewed." (I, pp. 23-4.)

As the dialogue with Caesonia continues, Caligula introduces another characteristically Gnostic theme, which recurs several times before the end of the play: the idea that men suffer evil because they are guilty. If the Gnostic "system" is to be logical with itself, all suffering must find an explanation. Rather than insist upon its mysteriousness, its absurdity, or its redemptive value in human life, the Gnostics, faithful to their need for logic and lucidity, could not make the supreme, transcendent God responsible for cosmic evil or human suffering. Suffering was either interpreted as a direct consequence of sin, or ascribed to the law of the conventional Archons, or *heimarméne.* [34] In *Christian Metaphysics,* Camus had remarked the tendency of some Gnostic writers (particularly Basilides) to underscore the gravity of human guilt, so as to make man entirely responsible for the evil he suffers in life. [35]

Caligula's pretention of being a transcendent divinity, *entirely innocent of the suffering he is inflicting,* his disparagement of human love as a "confining" emotion, inimical to both freedom and life; his conviction that love and bondage are a proof that the soul is *guilty* and unliberated — these ideas are in keeping with all Gnostic attitudes:

CAESONIA

... Surely you won't go back on love!

---

[34] The conventional gods in *Caligula* correspond to the Archons of the Gnostic cosmology. Cf. H. Jonas, *op. cit.,* p. 43: "The universe, the domain of the Archons, is like a vast prison whose innermost dungeon is the earth, the scene of man's life. ... The Archons collectively rule over the world, and each individually in his sphere is a warden of the cosmic prison. Their tyrannical world-rule is called *heimarméne,* universal Fate, a concept taken over from astrology, but now tinged with the gnostic anti-cosmic spirit."

[35] A. Camus, *Métaphysique Chrétienne...,* in *Essais,* pp. 1253-54: "Eloigné de toute spéculation, [Basilide] ne s'attache qu'au problème moral .... Ce qui l'intéresse c'est le péché et le côté humain des problèmes. ... Selon lui, il n'est pas de souffrance inutile. Et chaque souffrance exige un péché précédent qui la légitime .... Le Christ n'échappe pas à la loi universelle du péché."

CALIGULA

... Love, Caesonia ... I've learned the truth about love; it's nothing, nothing! .... I know what I'm talking about — and I invite you to the most gorgeous of shows, a sight for gods to gloat on, a whole world called to judgment. But for that I must have a crowd — spectators, victims, criminals, hundreds and thousands of them .... Let the accused come forward. I want my criminals, *and they are all criminals* .... (I, pp. 24-5.)

* * *

Act II dramatizes the consequences of Caligula's having set his Gnostic plan into execution. Dramatically, this act marks a clear progression over the first: the conspiracy against Caligula is rapidly mounted, and it is only a matter of time before the monster is to be brought down. Thematically, however, the second act merely re-echoes the first. The radically acosmic nature of Caligula's project is particularly evident in the scene at Cherea's house. The Patricians have met there to plan Caligula's assassination; and the pettiness of their grievances against the emperor provides a comic indication that they have missed the point of his metaphysical revolution. One Patrician is indignant because Caligula has humiliated him; a second wishes to avenge a murdered father; a third cannot forvige Caligula for making him a cuckold; a fourth is joining the conspiracy to recover a confiscated property. The Patricians, in short, though aristocratic in name, are hopelessly middle-class in their responses: unable to conceive a problem in anything but juridical and moralistic terms. As the First Patrician asserts, quite pompously, "our ruling motive is of a moral order." (II, p. 31) The Patricians have failed to understand that Caligula's revolution is neither social, nor economic, but primarily ontological: it is aimed at the destruction of Being itself. Cherea, who three years earlier had foreseen Caligula's new intellectual orientation, decides to join the conspiracy, despite the conspirators' petty motives. But he adds a warning: "You haven't taken your enemy's measure; that's obvious, since you attribute petty motives to him. But there's nothing petty about Caligula .... He's putting his power at the service of a loftier, deadlier passion, and it imperils everything we hold most sacred. True, it's not the first time Rome has seen a man wielding unlimited power; but it's the first time he sets no limit to his use of it, and counts mankind, and the world we know, for nothing. That's what appals me in Caligula; that's what I want to fight." (II, pp. 29-30.)

Cherea is being quite literal when he equates a denial of limit with a negation of man and the world. The aim of Caligula's politics is not political but metaphysical: "It imperils everything we hold must sacred." (II, p. 29.) Cherea joins the conspiracy, therefore, not to prevent the destruction of the State, so much as to combat Caligula's philosophy of destruction: "No, if I join forces with you, it's to combat a big idea —an ideal, if you like— whose triumph would mean the end of everything. I can endure your being made a mock of, but I cannot endure Caligula's carrying out his theories to the end. He is converting his philosophy into corpses and — unfortunately for us — it's a philosophy that's logical from start to finish." (II, p. 30.)

But a metaphysics of destruction cannot be destroyed at the height of its power. It must first run its course to the logical limit when, having nothing else to destroy, it turns against itself: "We must take action, I agree. But a frontal attack's quite useless when one is fighting an imperial madman in the full flush of his power.... You can only urge it on to follow its bent, and bide your time until its logic founders in sheer lunacy." (Id.)

In the final scene of Act II Caligula tells the young poet Scipio, whose father he has murdered, that "the same eternal truths appeal to us both." (II, p. 48.) He says this, however, in a moment of tenderness and of nostalgia for Being. What Caligula fears most in the young Scipio is not his hatred, but, in a literal sense, his "poetic" power, his power to create. As Cherea is a philosopher intent on salvaging the world of essence, Scipio is a poet capable of creating essence through his own powers. Caligula's "tender" scene with Scipio might be described, therefore, as a momentary lapse of Gnostic faith. In a fleeting vision, he realizes that the reality of the World is so overwhelming that he will never succeed in destroying it entirely, though he knows that it will never sate his appetite for infinity:

SCIPIO

All I know is that everything I feel or think of turns to love.

CALIGULA

... That, Scipio, is a privilege of noble hearts — and how I wish I could share your ... your limpidity! But my appetite for life's too keen; Nature can never sate it. You

belong to quite another world, and you can't understand.
You are single-minded for good; and I am single-minded
— for evil. (II, p. 49.)

Never during the play will Caligula's radical dualism ever be expressed more clearly than this. Never will his appraisal of the overwhelming power of life and Nature be more sober. Caligula visibly
senses that his Gnostic project is doomed. In playing the game of
poetry with Scipio, he has almost become ensnared by his latent love
for life and harmony. He realizes that the pure, sterile state of non-
being is neither metaphysically plausible nor politically attainable, for
even a politics of destruction carries behind it a burden of memory.

In admitting that the burden of memory is indestructible, Caligula
introduces another theme that was current among the early Gnostic
writers, namely, the idea that, willy-nilly, mankind is engaged in a
historical process. Man carries within himself the memory of the
corpses he has strewn behind. Where there is an indelible memory
of the past, there is history, and living in metaphysical isolation is
consequently impossible. In *Christian Metaphysics* Camus had summarized the Gnostic sense of history in the following way: "Another
influencial Gnostic theme, less vivid but equally true, is a sense of
history, that is, the idea that the world is headed towards a goal, as
it is the conclusion of a tragedy. The world is a starting point, it
had a beginning. Truths are not to be contemplated. We are acting
them out, and our salvation is at stake." [36]

---

[36] *Ibid.*, p. 1265. For a better understanding of this theme, cf. H. Jonas,
«Delimitation of the Gnostic Phenomenon," in *Le Origini dello Gnosticismo,
Colloquio de Messina 13-18 Aprile 1966* (Leiden, 1967), p. 98. The Gnostic
conception of history, according to Jonas, is "a conception of *human history*
as the growing ingression of knowledge in the generations of man, and this
requires *revelation* as a necessary vehicle of its progress. ... Gnosticism indeed
conceived of one pervading pattern and meaning of world history, with a
definite goal and a particular mode of progress. Contrary to Jewish apocalyp-
tics, kingdoms and nations have no place in it, only souls."
How does this Gnostic conception of history apply to *Caligula?* Though
Caligula's impossible vision is anti-cosmic, the emperor realizes that the realization of this vision can only take place in human time. In characteristic
Gnostic fashion, Caligula's conception of history has "a pervading pattern
and a particular mode of progress." His conception is also entirely personal.
History means essentially the progress of his own vision. Other men, other
empires have nothing to do with it. Everything in the objective sphere is of
equal importance, or unimportance.

The theme of "immersion in history" is the most discreetly treated in the play, yet it is present in this scene. Caligula's discovery of "the load of the future and the past" is one with his realization that he is immersed in a tragedy; and his discovery of tragedy is an implicit realization that Being will triumph over his vow of cosmic destruction: "Always we are attended by the same load of the future and the past. Those we have killed are always with us. But *they* are no great trouble. It's those we have loved, those who loved us and whom we did not love; regrets, desires, bitterness and sweetness, whores and gods, the gang celestial. . . . Solitude? No, Scipio, mine is full of gnashings of teeth, hideous with jarring sounds and voices." (II, p. 50.)

* * *

The bizarre adoration of Caligula-Venus, at the start of Act III, has some historical verisimilitude, if one is to believe Suetonius. [37] From another perspective, however, it might be interpreted both as a comic dramatization of the Gnostic idea of the Christian Incarnation, and as a parody of a Gnostic hymn.

Camus had remarked in his student essay that some of the Gnostics interpreted the role of Christ as that of a liberator sent by the superior God to combat the "bellicose and cruel" god of the lower world, and to liberate man from his clutches. Màrcion, in particular, thought of Jesus as a "revolutionary," an "emancipator," "the agent of a metaphysical coup d'état." [38] While, therefore, it would be wrong to suggest that Camus *intended* the adoration of Caligula-Venus as

---

But in the personal sphere, Caligula is caught in a process which began at a precise moment ("Je ne le savais pas *auparavant. Maintenant,* je sais.), and which end with the annihilation of his person ("qu'il est amer d'avoir raison et de devoir aller jusq'à la consommation. Car j'ai peur de la consommation").

[37] The historical Caligula arrogated to himself the majesty of the gods; replaced the heads of the gods with simulacra of his own on public statues; and, in the temple of Castor and Pollux, he would often stand "inter fratres deos" to offer himself to the adoration of passers-by. (Suetonius, *Caligula,* XXII, in *op. cit.,* p. 77.)

[38] A. Camus, *Métaphysique Chrétienne . . . ,* in *Essais,* pp. 1256-57: "On voit déjà quelle importance va revêtir le Christ [pour Marcion]. Il n'est rien de moins que *l'envoyé* du Dieu suprême pour combattre le Dieu méchant, créateur du monde, et délivrer l'homme de sa domination. Jésus accomplit ici-bas une *mission révolutionnaire. Emancipateur autant que Rédempteur, il est l'organe d'une sorte de coup d'Etat métaphysique."

a Gnostic dramatization of Christ's liberating mission, it is unquestionable that the scene has a Gnostic resonance. Caligula assumes a divine form in order to liberate men from the dominion of the evil, conventional gods. That this is the "serious" intent of his buffoonery becomes clear when he confides to Scipio: "If you don't mind, that will remain our secret — the great enigma of our reign [i.e. that Caligula is "envious of the gods"]. Really, you know, there's only one thing for which I might be blamed today — and that's this small advance I've made upon the path of freedom. For someone who loves power the rivalry of the gods is rather irksome. Well, I've proved to these imaginary gods that any man, without previous training, if he applies his mind to it, can play their absurd parts to perfection.... I've ... realized that there's only one way of getting even with the gods. All that's needed is to be as cruel as they. (III, p. 57.)

Caligula, as reigning divinity, has the power of assuming any divine form so as to combat the cruel and illusory Archons of the lower world. Caligula's desire to destroy both the physical world and its ruling Archons is consistent both with his purpose and with the traditional Gnostic cosmogony. If only other mortals might realize, like their Gnostic mentor, that they might put an end to the traditional domination of the conventional gods by becoming superior to them! "Any man ... if he applies his *mind* to it, can play their absurd parts to perfection." To achieve such an apotheosis, nothing else is required except an ascetic affirmation of will, and a transcendence of the conventional concept of *heimarméne,* as it is understood by those still imprisoned in the snare of matter and psyche: "There's no understanding Fate; therefore I choose to play the part of Fate. I wear the foolish, unintelligible face of a professional god. And that is what the men who were here with you have learned to adore.... The great mistake you people make is not to take the drama [of superior knowledge] seriously enough. If you did, you'd know that any man can play lead in the divine comedy and become a god. All he needs to do is to harden his heart." (III, p. 59.) Is the tenor of Caligula's rebellion so far different from that of Marcion?

The litanies recited in honor of Caligula, in the same scene, bear a curious resemblance to certain Gnostic hymns, some of which Camus might have read. (They are also, quite clearly, a pastiche of the litanies in honor of the Virgin.) As recited by both Caesonia and the Patricians, the prayer to Caligula can be reconstituted as follows:

Our Lady of pangs and pleasures,
Born of the waves, bitter and bright with seafoam,
O Queen whose gifts are laughter and regrets,
Rancours and raptures,
Teach us the indifference that kindles love anew,
Make known to us the truth about this world —
    which is that it has none,
And grant us strength to live up to this verity of
    verities.
Bestow your gifts on us,
And shed on our faces the light of your impartial
    cruelty, your wanton hatred;
Unfold above our eyes your arms laden with flowers
    and murders,
Welcome your wandering children home,
To the bleak sanctuary of your heartless, thankless love.
Give us your passions without object, your griefs
    devoid of reason,
Your raptures that lead nowhere.
O Queen, so empty yet so ardent, inhuman yet
    so earthly,
Make us drunk with the wine of your equivalence,
And surfeit us for ever in the brackish darkness
    of your heart. (III, pp. 52-55.)

With the rhythms and images of Camus' prayer still fresh in one's mind, one might consider a Gnostic hymn drawn at random from the *Corpus Hermeticum*:

> We thank thee, with our whole soul and our whole heart stretched out to thee, ineffable Name ... that thou hast shown to all of us fatherly goodness, love and kindness, and an even sweeter power in bestowing on us by thy grace mind, speech, gnosis: mind, that we think thee, speech, that we praise thee, gnosis, that in thy knowledge we rejoice.
>
> Saved by thy light, we rejoice that thou hast shown thyself to us whole, we rejoice that thou hast made us gods while still in our bodies through the vision of thee.
>
> Man's only thank-offering to thee is to know thy greatness. We came to know thee, O light of human life, we came to know thee, O light of all gnosis, we have come to know thee, O womb impregnated by the seed of the Father . . . .

In adoration of thy grace, we ask no other grace but that thou shoulds preserve us in thy gnosis and that we shall not stumble from the life so gained. [39]

Camus was unquestionably aware of the *Corpus Hermeticum,* though it is difficult to ascertain whether he was familiar with it. [40] It is interesting, in any case, to compare the style, the vision, the rhythm and the tone of Caesonia's litany with those of the Gnostic hymn. In both cases, the invocations are highly emotional, incantatory, and repetitious:

Caligula	*Corpus Hermeticum*
Our Lady of pangs... O Queen... O Queen so empty....	O light of human life... O light of all gnosis... O womb....

Both prayers make use of characteristic verbs, whether in the imperative or the past indicative:

teach us... make *known* to us... grant us... bestow your gifts on us... shed on our faces... unfold... welcome... give... make... surfeit us....	thout hast shown... thou hast made... to *know* thy greatness... we came to *know* thee... we have come to *know* thee... we ask... preserve us....

In both texts, the divinity is described with a striking sexual metaphor:

Our Lady of pangs and pleasures, Born of the waves....	O womb impregnated by the seed of the Father....

The suppliant's relation to the divinity is that of the insignificant child to a powerful, distant, awesome parent:

Welcome your wandering children home....	... thou hast shown to all of us fatherly goodness... preserve us... that we shall not stumble....

---

[39] Quoted in H. Jonas, *op. cit.,* pp. 287-89. This is the final prayer of the *Logos Teleios* by the pseudo-Apuleius, in *Asclepius 41.*

[40] It is likely that he had not. Camus obtained his knowledge of Gnostic writings principally through intermediate sources (cf. the bibliography of *Christian Metaphysics,* in *Essais,* p. 1311). The only Gnostic texts he seems to have consulted directly are those contained in Tertullian, *De Praescriptionibus adv. Haereses, Adversus Marcionem,* and *Adversus Valentiniarum.* in the Migne edition (*Ibid.*)

In both cases, the divinity is best described in negative terms:

Your *heartless, thankless* love ... your passions *without object,* your griefs *devoid* of reason ... your raptures that lead *nowhere* ... O Queen, so *empty* ... *inhuman*	... thee, *ineffable* Name ....

The suppliant's commitment to the divinity, in both instances, is total, uncompromising, and bacchic:

Make us drunk ... and surfeit us	... our *whole* soul and our *whole* heart *streched out* ... in adoration of thy grace ....

In both prayers, man and the physical universe are esteemed insignificant:

Make known to us the truth about this world ... which is *that it has* *none*	thou hast made us *gods while* *still in our bodies* ... no other grace but that thou shouldst pre- serve us in thy gnosis ....

Finally, perhaps most significantly, the suppliant, in both prayers, is either asking the divinity to favor him with an essential, secret, and supremely significant truth, or thanking the divinity for having so favored him:

Make known to us the truth about this world ... this verity of ve- rities ... the bleak sanctuary	the vision of thee ... we came to *know* thee [thrice repeated] ... preserve us in thy gnosis ....

In the light of these comparisons it seems reasonable to suggest that Caesonia's prayer contains unmistakable Gnostic resonances. [41]

The dialogue between Cherea and Caligula, later in Act III, contains the final and most dramatic philosophical confrontation between Hellenism and Gnosticism. In a discussion revolving about the central issues of truth and falsehood, the central topic is whether truth is

---

[41] Particularly Gnostic is its emphasis on the nothingness of the world, and on the necessity of arriving at a *gnōsis* of this truth: "Instruis-nous de la vérité de ce monde qui est de n'en point avoir / Et accorde-nous la force de vivre à la hauteur de cette vérité sans égale." (Original text)

essentially a liberation from limit (Caligula's *gnōsis*), or a submission to it (Cherea's Hellenic notion of truth). Cherea declares that he cannot approve of Caligula's "illogical" attempt to reconcile reason with a denial of limit. *Lógos* and *ápeiron*, declares Cherea, are mutually exclusive notions, and Caligula's attempt to infuse one into the other is "noxious and cruel:"

CALIGULA

Then why wish to kill me?

CHEREA

I've told you why; because I regard you as noxious, a constant menace. I like, and need, to feel secure. So do most men. They resent living in a world where the most preposterous fancy may at any moment become a reality, and the absurd transfix their lives, like a dagger in the heart. I feel as they do; I refuse to live in a topsy-turvy world. I want to know where I stand, and to stand secure.

"Security and logic don't go together," replies Caligula. He is obviously using the word "logic" in an un-Hellenic sense, for it was not characteristic of the Greeks (as Camus frequently remarked) to push any idea to the point of vindictiveness or exaggeration. [42] The desire to infuse total clarity into a universe which, by its very nature, is composed of light and shadow, is more of a Gnostic than a Greek ambition: "... what I want is to live and be happy. Neither, to my mind, is possible if one pushes the absurd to its logical conclusion. As you see, I'm quite an ordinary sort of man. True, there are moments when, to feel free of them, I desire the death of those I love, or I hanker after women from whom the ties of family or friendship debar me. Were logic everything, I'd kill or fornicate on such occasions. But I consider that these passing fancies have no great importance. If everyone set to gratifying them, the world would be impossible to live in, and happiness, too, would go by the board. And these, I repeat, are the things that count, for me." (III, pp. 67-8.)

* * *

[42] E.g., A. Camus, *L'Homme Révolté*, in *Essais*, pp. 438-40: "Les Grecs n'enveniment rien. Dans leurs audaces les plus extrêmes, ils restent fidèles à cette mesure, qu'ils avaient déifiée. ... Les Grecs n'ont jamais fait de la pensée ... un camp retranché ...."

The final act of the play appears to contain and recapitulate all the Gnostic themes that have previously been discussed: the evil nature of the physical world; the ubiquitousness of guilt; the moral ideal of rebellious asceticism; the nostalgia for a "superior" world of perfection and purity; the desire for liberation through knowledge; the realization that life is essentially tragic, that it is "falling off" from an aboriginally pure and superior state, that an awareness of history is contemporaneous with an awareness of tragedy.

Two scenes stand out in a particular way. The poetry contest is a comic *trouvaille,* but its theatrical originality should not obscure the presence of several Gnostic ideas, some of which have appeared before. Caligula, it will be remembered, dislikes poets because they tell the supreme lie of endowing Nature with value. Because they can speak of death in nothing but the tritest poetic terms, each of the poets is immediately interrupted by Caligula. Scipio is the only poet who knows the truth about death: "You're very young to understand Death's lessons," Caligula tells him. Significantly enough, Scipio speaks of death as a liberation, a *regressus animae,* a pursuit of purification, a point on which both Gnosticism and Neoplatonism were in agreement:

> Pursuit of happiness that purifies the heart,
> Skies rippling with light,
> O wild, sweet, festal joys, frenzy without hope!
>
> (III, p. 86.)

As the scene ends, Caligula chases the poets from the room, and purifies his Gnostic republic of their lies by forcing them to lick their slates clean.

In the final scene of the play, Caligula kills Caesonia, then himself. Being flesh-born, Caesonia is impure and guilty. She must die. Since the start of the play, Caligula's sexual behavior has been perfectly consistent with his superior vision. He has repeatedly refused Caesonia's body, and has made his brief affair with Mucius' wife a mere expression of his contempt and hatred of the world. He has carried Caesonia around like a corpse to be soon disposed of, a horrifying obstacle between him and total purity: "This purity you talk of — every man acquires it, in his own way. Mine has been to follow the essential to the end." (III, pp. 88-89.) Though she has remained in Caligula's company, Caesonia has retained a fundamentally Hellenic vision of the world. She continues to believe in life, love, and the "happiness that does not thrive on bloodshed." (III, p. 92.) Killing his *alter ego* is the step that must logically precede Caligula's own destruction. Caligula must be alone in knowing that happiness resides beyond the frontier of the physical universe; that it is derived from a *gnosis* that is above pain: "Beyond the frontier of pain lies a splendid, sterile happiness. But for this freedom, I'd have been a contented man. Thanks to it, I have won the godlike enlightenment of the solitary." (III, pp. 92-3.)

Caesonia is despatched because, bearing the mark of the universal condition, she was "guilty" of existing. If Caligula's solitary enlightenment is to be totally "godlike," he, too, must disappear: "There's nothing in this world, or in the other, made to my stature. And yet I know, and you too know (*still weeping, he stretches out his arms towards the mirror*) that all I need is for the impossible to be. The impossible! I've searched for it at the confines of the world . . . ." (III, p. 94.)

But the Gnostic project is a failure. The annihilation of matter does *not* transform the psyche into spirit. Destruction added to destruction yields but a total of destruction. Caligula's death brings not a liberation, but a cumulative conviction of guilt. His final cry, "To history, Caligula! Go down to history," is an acknowledgment that "we are attended by the same load of the future and the past." Caligula, like Marcion, realizes that the universe is necessarily "oriented towards a destined goal, as it is the conclusion of a tragedy."

* * *

It has been the purpose of this chapter to suggest that some of the major themes of *Caligula* are a dramatic projection of Camus' research on Gnosticism in the second chapter of *Christian Metaphysics*. The suggestion may still appear insufficient or unconvincing; and, even if the author had proved his point, the reader might reasonably be tempted to object: "What dimension can the use of such an esoteric category as 'Gnosticism' possibly add to one's comprehension of the play? Is it not to confuse the issue to use such an ancient and obscure system of thought to explicate a work that is far more easily understood on its own terms?"

Although such an objection is well-founded, the advantages of reading the text of *Caligula* from a Gnostic perspective are not by any means negligible. Such a reading gives the play an even wider philosophical resonance than it would have if explicated, say, from an exclusively phenomenological or existential point of view. The play also acquires a greater historic depth. The ideology of the play appears as deeply rooted in Greco-Roman literature as are its characters and its incidents.

Caligula deals neither with exclusively modern obsessions, nor with exclusively Gnostic themes; but it does deal with ideas and themes which first appeared in the Gnostic literature of the early Christian era. These ideas can be said not only to be relevant to the modern temper, but even to coincide so singularly with it that it does not appear an exaggeration to call them "forerunners of modern nihilism."

Caligula also succeeds in attesting to an inner cohesion in the development of Camus' philosophical interests, and to a harmony of his thought and his sensibility. Problems once treated by a young academic mind later, and quite unconsciously, find their way into theatrical form. Far from pointing to some exotic or escapist fancy, Camus' interest in Gnosticism seems in keeping with his most besetting preoccupations. In *Christian Metaphysics*, he had hinted at the "résonance toute moderne" of some of the Gnostic tenets. [43] That he chose to write a "diplôme" that would oblige him to read Gnostic sources, at a time when he is known to have been reading Marx, Nietzsche, and Heidegger, indicates that he must have previously sensed the affinities between the Marcions of the second century and those of the twentieth. It is plausible, in fact, to assume that Camus' interest in Gnosticism was fostered by his prior interest in existentialist thought. Hans Jonas writes of his own "evolution of interest from Heidegger to Gnosticism:"

> When, many years ago, I turned to the study of Gnosticism, I found that the viewpoints, the optics as it were, which I had acquired in the school of Heidegger enabled me to see aspects of Gnostic thought that had been missed before....

---

[43] A. Camus, *Métaphysique Chrétienne* ..., in *Essais*, p. 1257: "Dans cette vue pessimiste sur le monde ... court la résonance d'une sensibilité toute moderne."

I am inclined to believe that it was the thrill of this dimly felt affinity which had lured me into the gnostic labyrinth in the first place. Then, after long sojourn in those distant lands returning to my own, the contemporary philosophic scene, I found that what I had learned out there made me now better understand the shore from which I had set out. The extended discourse with ancient nihilism proved ... a help in discerning and placing the meaning of modern nihilism. [44]

A second objection to the present chapter might be phrased as follows: "Granted that many of the themes in *Caligula* resemble those in Camus' chapter on Gnosticism, just how solid is the chapter in the first place? Can Camus' ideas on Gnosticism really be taken seriously when Gnosticism is known to be an elusive, Proteus-like movement, whose very significance is open to academic debate?"

Camus' analysis of Gnosticism has its obvious limitations: he collected and summarized whatever information was available in the early thirties. His sources — De Faye and Amelineau, in particular — are slightly dated, though certainly not discredited; and though he never consulted Harnack on the subject of Gnosticism, he wrote at a time when Harnack's definition of Gnosticism as "an acute Hellenization of Christianity" was still prevalent. [45] Subsequent research, particularly that of Professor Jonas, has indicated that Gnosticism was far more than "a Hellenic reflection on Christian themes" — indeed, that in some cases Gnosticism was not affected by either Hellenic or Christian modes of thought:

The genuine theoretical aspirations revealed in the higher type of gnostic speculation, bearing out as it seemed the testimony of the early Church Fathers, led Adolph von Harnack to his famous formulation that Gnosticism was "the acute Hellenization of Christianity," while the slower and more measured evolution of orthodox theology was to be regarded as its "chronic Hellenization . . . ." Perspicacious as this diagnosis is, as a definition of Gnosticism it falls short in both the terms that make up the formula, "Hellenization" and

[44] H. Jonas, "Epilogue: Gnosticism, Existentialism, and Nihilism," in *op. cit.*, p. 320.

[45] Harnack's formulation was generally accepted until subsequent research on Gnosticism, especially after 1945, established the originality of the Gnostic phenomenon. (H. Jonas, *op. cit.*, pp. 36-37).

"Christianity." It treats Gnosticism as a solely Christian phenomenon, whereas subsequent research has established its wider range; and it gives way to the Hellenic appearance of gnostic conceptualization and of the concept of *gnosis* itself, which in fact only thinly disguises a heterogeneous spiritual substance. It is the *genuineness,* i.e. the *underivative nature,* of this *substance* that defeats all attempts at derivation that concern more than the outer shell of expression . . . . [46]

Camus did consult the authoritative French sources of his day. He assimilated them well, though perhaps too hastily, and summarized their findings with an acceptable accuracy. Frequently he went so far as to copy entire passages and quotations and to pass them off, unwittingly or not, as his own. *Habent sua fata libelli.*

So far as one unspecialized reader is able to judge, Camus' information was accurate, if limited. His solitary discourse with Valentinus, Marcion, and Basilides, in his early twenties, most certainly helped him clarify and define his own meanings, values, and obsessions. Their pessimism, their rebelliousness, their arrogant asceticism, were to leave a deep impression, perhaps deeper in fact than that made by any other ideological movement in Antiquity. The seeds of Gnosticism, enriched by the ferment of modern philosophy, were later to bear fruit.

---

[46] *Ibid.*

CHAPTER IV

THE PRESENCE OF AUGUSTINE

The fourth and final chapter of *Christian Metaphysics and Neo-platonism* is devoted to an analysis of Augustinian thought. [1] Camus opens with a reference to Augustine's ardent and tormented personality, betraying his sympathy for the man he once called "that other African," whose temperament he seems to grasp intuitively. Is Camus speaking of himself or of Augustine, for example, when he writes: "A passionate, sensual person, his fear of being incapable of observing continence long made him put off his conversion. At the same time, he had a taste for rational truth .... But ... he was obsessed by the problem of evil: 'I sought to know from whence evil came, and could find no way out.' And he is pursued by the spectre of death: 'I was gnawed by the fear of dying without having discovered the truth.' Greek in his need for coherence, Christian in his spiritual anxieties, he long remained at a distance from Christianity." [2] Is this not an excellent summary of Camus' own moral and intellectual obsessions? Did Camus not say of himself in later years: "My preoccupations are Christian, but my nature is pagan"? [3] And elsewhere: "I am not a Christian ... My heart is Greek." [4]

---

[1] A. Camus, *Métaphysique Chrétienne et Néoplatonisme,* in *Essais d'Al-bert Camus,* ed. R. Quilliot (Paris, 1965), pp. 1293-1309.

[2] *Ibid.,* pp. 1294-5 Compare the following description of Camus' "obsessions" by Gabriel Marcel: "He knows, or thinks he knows, that a religious solution is unacceptable to him. His stumbling-block, like that of so many other writers, is the mystery of evil." (G. Marcel, *Les débuts de la saison théâtrale,* in *Etudes* [Jan., 1946], v. 248, p. 109).

[3] A. Camus, *Interview de Stockholm,* in *Essais,* p. 1615.

[4] A. Camus, *Actuelles I,* in *Essais,* p. 380.

The chapter on Augustine dates back to 1936. Fifteen years later, almost at the pinnacle of his literary glory, Camus lists Augustine among the first of a long line of literary figures to come from North Africa: "In ... North Africa ... there is literary an efflorescence [of modern authors] .... Fruits grow fast in that land. Of course, it was Saint Augustine's homeland." [5] Saint Augustine thus makes occasional appearances throughout Camus' literary production, somewhat like those isolated phrases with recur throughout a musical work and endow the separate movements with a discreet unity. Camus, who might reasonably be considered one of the most "actual" of contemporary French authors, thus never seems to have forgotten the spiritual itinerary of that "other African," distant in time but close in spirit, who spent a lifetime wrestling with the problems which, fifteen centuries later, he still considered relevant.

How and where does Augustine appear in Camus' literary production? Can one speak of an Augustinian influence on his thinking?

I. *"Christian Metaphysics"*

Camus places the Augustinian system (historically) at the terminal point of a "common evolution" of Greek and Christian thought. [6] During the first three centuries, Christianity had sought to "adapt its system of dogmas to its original religious life until the moment when its meeting with Neoplatonism provided it with a metaphysical framework already molded by a religious thought, ... and it blossomed into a second revelation, Augustinian thought." [7] Camus' analysis of Augustine's ideas is divided into three parts, entitled, respectively: "Augustine's psychological experience and Neoplatonism;" "The Relations of Hellenism to Christianity;" "The Problem of Faith and Reason." Part Two, in turn, has to two subdivisions, the first bearing upon the problems of Evil, Grace, and Freedom; the second upon Augustine's teaching on the Logos and the Trinity.

Part one begins with an evaluation of the "dosage" of Neoplatonism contained in Augustine's works. After comparing a number of Au-

---

[5] A. Camus, *Les Nouvelles Littéraires*, May 10, 1951, in *Essais*, p. 1342.
[6] A. Camus, *Métaphysique Chrétienne et Néoplatonisme*, in *Essais*, p. 1230.
[7] *Ibid.*

gustinian texts with similar texts from Plotinus, Camus suggests that Augustine's reading of the *Enneads* provided him with a philosophical doctrine of the Word (Logos), which he could relate to St. John's Prologue. He adds that Augustine gave Plotinus' doctrine of the Logos an entirely Christian "twist," as the second hypostasis of Plotinus became, in Augustine's system, the Word made Flesh. [8]

The most constant obsession of Augustine's life and work (Camus continues) was the problem of Evil, an obsession which sustained him in his passionate search for solutions, first in Manichean philosophy, then in Neoplatonism, finally in the Gospel. At the end of his intellectual itinerary, Augustine realized that "the solution did not reside in knowledge, that the solution to his doubts and to his disgust for the flesh was not to be found in intellectual evasion but in a total consciousness of his deprivation and misery." [9] Augustine is indebted to Plotinus, both for his doctrine of the Word as Mediator between man and God, and for his solution to the problem of Evil. The former doctrine enabled Augustine to understand the "destiny" of Christ as the Word of God, the latter to realize that Evil is "linked to matter," and that its reality is "wholly negative." [10] "Suddenly all of Saint Augustine's doubts seemed over; but his conversion did not immediately follow. A curious feature of Augustine's personality is that his experience always remains the reference of his intellectual research. Satisfied but unconvinced, he himself remarks that Neoplatonism could give him everything except the Incarnation and personal humility. Only when he had understood this was he delivered, in the garden of his home, by an explosion of tears and joy. It was an almost physical conversion, so all-encompassing that Augustine progressively gave up all that had previously given his life its meaning, in order to dedicate himself to God." [11] This paragraph brings the first part of Camus' analysis to a close.

In part two, he considers several issues on which Hellenism and Christianity either concur or conflict. What are the Augustinian "solutions" to the problems of Evil, Grace, Freedom? Natural evil "is justified somewhat like the dark areas in a painting." As for moral evil, "the question is more complex, since sin, a consequence of the

---

[8] *Ibid.*, p. 1294.
[9] *Ibid.*, p. 1295.
[10] *Ibid.*, p. 1296.
[11] *Ibid.*

original fall, is imputable to us." [12] Camus is visibly impressed by the indispensable rôle attributed to Grace in the Augustinian scheme. Deprived of divine aid, man is incapable of meriting salvation by his own means. The natural virtues of the "good pagans," for example, were given them in order to incite Christians to emulate them. Whoever boasts of his natural virtues can even transform them into so many vices. Divine grace, being entirely gratuitous, cannot be merited by man's own means. Faith in God is already the beginning of grace. Of Augustine's rigorous system, Camus remarks: "One sees the extremes to which Augustine can go in his thinking. He never avoids any of the difficulties of a problem. Of course, there seems to be no problem where nothing except human submission is involved. This absolute dependence [of man on God], however, as might be expected where evil is concerned, raises major difficulties. If divine grace is absolutely arbitrary, if man can do nothing save trust in God, is it possible to speak of human freedom? Our one freedom is precisely our capacity to do evil. Augustine's last word on this vital Christian problem is an avowal of ignorance. God's freedom to act arbitrarily remains intact." [13]

Several pages follow on Augustine's attitude towards the Pelagian heresy. Pelagius' contention that man is free to do either good or evil, that grace is but a help "ad facilius operandum," meets with Augustine's disapproval: "Original sin destroyed man's capacity not to sin .... Scripture is explicit on this point, which Augustine underscores. Human nature is vitiated by sin and, were it not for baptism, man would be doomed to perdition .... The universal desolation of the world, and the misery of our condition (graphically drawn by Augustine) are a proof of our fallen state .... " [14] The first logical consequence of original sin is damnation, which is theoretically universal. Man's only hope is in God's mercy. A second consequence, which Camus considered one of the most inhuman of Augustine's teachings, is the damnation of unbaptized children. [15]

After examining the problems of Sin, Grace, and Freedom, Camus proceeds to a consideration of the Augustinian teachings on the Logos

---

[12] *Ibid.*, p. 1297.
[13] *Ibid.*, p. 1298.
[14] *Ibid.*, p. 1300.
[15] *Ibid.*, p. 1301.

and the Trinity. His analysis, at this point, contains several curious misinterpretations. Quite accurately, he points out that Saint Augustine discovered in Neoplatonism "a certain conception of the Word." The essential difference, he continues, between the Augustinian and Plotinian doctrines of the Word is that the latter "establishes a hierarchy of hypostases and emphasizes the distance that separates the One from the Logos," while Augustine considers God "not as the source of the other essences, but of the One Nature of the Trinity." [16] Camus concludes that the Augustinian doctrine of the Trinity might be summarized in the following terms: "The three Persons are, therefore, identical. Three basic conclusions follow: the three Persons have but one will and one operation: 'Ubi nullam naturam [sic] esse, nulla est diversitas voluntatum.' 'It is not the Word alone who appeared on earth, but the entire Trinity.' In the Incarnation of the Son, the entire Trinity is united to a human body." [17]

In this, perhaps the most confusing passage of *Christian Metaphysics*, theological fact can hardly be distinguished from misinterpretation and sheer fantasy. Most of the confusion, as I shall later explain, can be attributed to a hasty spoliation of one of Camus' sources. [18]

In the third and final part of his analysis, bearing upon the alleged "conflict" between Faith and Reason in Augustine's work, Camus presents a rather hasty summary of Augustine's "solution," and underscores the importance of this "solution" in the history of Western thought: "Reason becomes more flexible. It is illumined by the light of Faith. Augustine's idea of faith, one must remember, presupposes both the adherence of the spirit to supernatural truths, and man's humble submission to the Grace of Christ." [19]

This "flexibility" of Augustinian reason — a point to which Camus reverts once again in his general conclusion — is presented as one of Augustine's main contributions to Western philosophy. What Camus seems to imply is that Augustine's philosophy represents the culmination of a progressive "compromise" between Hellenic reason and Christian faith:

[16] *Ibid.*, p. 1303.
[17] *Ibid.*
[18] See my analysis of Camus' method, *infra*, pp. 185-95.
[19] A. Camus, *Métaphysique Chrétienne et Néoplatonisme,* in *Essais,* p. 1305.

Saint Augustine enables one to understand what the evolution of Christianity had accomplished: it had rendered Greek reason progressively flexible and had incorporated it into its edifice, in an enclosure within which it became harmless. Once within this enclosure, reason was forced to capitulate. In this regard, Augustine uses Neoplatonism to bolster a doctrine of humility and faith. His role in the evolution of Christianity was to facilitate the relaxation of reason, to turn Socratic logic towards religious speculation, and to transmit this already fashioned tool to the Fathers of the Christian Church.

In this sense, it is possible to consider Augustinism as a "second revelation," a Christian metaphysics erected upon an evangelical faith. The miracle is that they are not contradictory. [20]

Augustine's role, therefore, was to "transform" the early Christian faith into a philosophy; to resolve the conflict between faith and reason by incorporating reason to faith; and to enrich the Christian faith with Greek thought without depriving it of its originality.

To this general conclusion Camus adds a final remark: "At the time of Saint Augustine's death, Christianity had risen to the status of a philosophy. Henceforth it was sufficiently armed to defend itself during the sinister period which was to follow. For many years, it remained the one common hope, the one effective shield against catastrophe in the West. Christian thought had thus conquered its universality. [21]

* * *

In order to determine to what extent Camus' analysis of the Augustinian "system" is based upon personal reflection and familiarity with original texts, I have investigated his use of secondary source materials, particularly those cited in his bibliography. The initial impression derived from the footnote references in chapter four is that Camus worked almost exclusively with primary sources. A perusal of his secondary sources makes it evident, however, that Camus' entire chapter is a hastily compiled and largely unavowed spoliation of previous research by Augustinian scholars. Camus seems to have done

---

[20] *Ibid.*, p. 1306.
[21] *Ibid.*, pp. 1309-10.

little, if any, reading of the primary texts. Words, sentences, entire paragraphs are taken from secondary sources without acknowledgement.

In the first part of the chapter, for example (considering the problem of Neoplatonic influences on Augustine), Camus begins by asserting that, in his works, Augustine "quotes several texts of the *Enneads*." [22] He then "sustains" his assertion with a list of references to Plotinus' work, which seems impressive in itself: (I, vi, *Du Beau*; III, vi, *De la Providence*; III, iv, *Du Démon qui nous est donné en partage*; IV, iii, *Questions sur l'âme*; VI, *Des trois hypostases principales*; V, vi, *Le principe supérieur à l'être qui ne pense pas*.) [23] This is a futile reference, both because it abstains from stating exactly what Augustine borrowed from these texts, and because it is not at all the result of Camus' personal research. It has simply been copied out of L. Grandgeorge's *Saint Augustine et le Néo-platonisme*, a source which Camus studiously avoids mentioning in his footnotes. [24]

Camus then states that "most suggestive anologies" can be drawn between Augustine's and Plotinus' ideas on the attributes of God: His ineffability, His eternity, His ubiquity, His spirituality.[25] Describing the "exuberant and voluptuous life" of Augustine at Carthage, Camus refers to the following text: "Salvien, *Degulernatore Dei* [sic], *Patrologie latine*, VII, 16-17: '... débordants de vices, bouillonants d'iniquité, des hommes engourdis par le vice et enflés de nourriture puaient la sale volupté." [26]

Several things about this reference are perplexing. The real title of Salvianus' work is *De Gubernatione Dei*, and it is to be found in Volume LIII of the Migne *Latin Patrology*. But why does Camus, referring to a Latin text, quote it in French? This is not a customary procedure with him. Quite by chance, one comes across the following reference to Salvianus in P. Alfaric's work, entitled *l'Evolution Intellectuelle de Saint Augustin*: "... je veux parler de Carthage. Je

---

[22] *Ibid.*, p. 1293.

[23] *Ibid.*

[24] L. Grandgeorge, *Saint Augustin et le Néo-Platonisme* (Paris, 1396), pp. 39-40. Camus gives no reference to this work in his footnotes, but he does include it in his bibliography.

[25] A. Camus, *Métaphysique Chrétienne...*, in *Essais*, p. 1293.

[26] *Ibid.*, p. 1293 sg.

la vois *débordante de vices, bouillonante d'iniquités,* pleine de gens mais plus encore de turpitudes, comblée de richesses mais surtout de vices. J'y vois des hommes plus criminels les uns que les autres ... ici engourdis par le vin et là gonflés de nourriture ... Tous ses ci-toyens puaient, pour ainsi dire, la sale volupté ... " [27]

Camus, one suspects, simply copied this text at random and oc-casionally inverted the word order so as to disguise his source. I am, in any case, convinced that Alfaric's book is the secret source of Camus' description of Carthage, since his erroneous reference to the Patrology (Vol. VII) simply duplicates an error commited by Alfaric himself. [28]

The second part of Camus' analysis is entitled "Hellenism and Christianity in Augustine." In this entire section, Camus indulges in a plundering of sources that is both systematic and unconfessed, as the following parallels will indicate.

His analysis of "natural" and "moral" evil is taken textually from Etienne Gilson's *Introduction à l'Etude de Saint Augustin.* [29] The concordance of language is irrefutable:

A. Camus (*Mét. Chrétienne,* in *Essais,* Paris, 1965).	E. Gilson (*Introduction...* Paris, 1929).
"Mais encore faut-il *distinguer* deux sortes de maux: le *mal na-turel...* et *le mal moral...*" [30]	"Il est bon de *distinguer* entre le *mal naturel* et *le mal moral.*" [31]
"*Comment Dieu* a-t-il pu nous *douer* d'un *libre arbitre, c'est-à-dire d'une volonté capable de faire le mal?*" [32]	"La question est donc de savoir *comment* un *Dieu* parfait a pu nous *douer du libre arbitre, c'est-à-dire d'une volonté capable de faire le mal?*" [33]

---

[27] P. Alfaric, *L'Evolution Intellectuelle de Saint Augustin* (Paris, 1918), p. 31. The *De Gubernatione Dei* is to be found in Vol. LIII and not in Vol. VII of the *Patrologia Latina,* as is erroneously indicated by Alfaric (See P. L. LIII, col. 143-4).

[28] A. Camus, *Métaphysique Chrétienne* ... , in *Essais,* p. 1294.

[29] E. Gilson. *Introduction à l'Etude de Saint Augustin* (Paris, 1929).

[30] A. Camus, *Métaphysique Chrétienne* ... , in *Essais,* p. 1297.

[31] E. Gilson, *op. cit.,* p. 180.

[32] A. Camus, *Métaphysique Chrétienne* ... , in *Essais,* p. 1297.

[33] E. Gilson, *op. cit.,* p. 181.

"Et nous sommes si profondément pervertis que c'est de Dieu seul *que vient tout bon usage du libre arbitre. Laissé à lui-même l'homme ne posséderait en propre* que la malfaisance, *le mensonge, et le péché:* "Nemo habet de sunisi [sic] mendacium atque peccatum." [Note 4, bottom of the page: *In Johan.* V, 1; P. L, 18 [sic]; t. 35: col. 414 [sic], et aussi *Sermo 156,* II, 12; P. L, t. 38: col. 856: "Cum dico tibi: Sine adjutorio Dei nihil agis nihil boni dico, nam ad male agendum habes sine adjutom [sic] Dei liberam voluntatem." [34]

"C'est ainsi *que les vertus des païens* sont inopérantes. *Dieu les leur* a données *pour nous inciter* à les avoir *si elles nous manquent,* et pour rabaisser notre orgueil *si nous les possédons* ... [Note 1, bottom of the page: *De civ. Dei* V, 18, 3; P. L, t. 41; vol. [sic] 165, *id.* V. 19, P. L, t. 41, col. 165-166; *Epist.* 138; III, 17; P. L, t. 33, col. 33 [sic]; *De Patientia* XXVII, 25; P. L, tome 40; col. 624. *De gratia christi,* XXIV, 25. P. L, t. 44. *Id.* 376 [sic].] "Plus encore, *ces vertus naturelles deviennent autant de vices* lorsque *l'homme s'en glorifie.* [Note 2, bottom of the page: *De civ. Dei* XXI, 16; P. L, t. 41; col. 730 et XIX, 25 chap., intitulé: "Quod non possint ibi veræ esse insutes [sic] uti non est vera religio." (t. 41, col. 56). Cf. aussi *De div.*

"C'est donc de lui que vient en général à l'homme *tout bon usage du libre arbitre; laissé à lui-même l'homme ne posséderait en propre* que le pouvoir de mal faire, *le mensonge et le péché.*" [Note 5, bottom of page: "Nemo habet de suo nisi mendacium atque peccatum." In Johan., V, 1; t. 35, col. 414 [sic]—"Cum dico tibi; sine adjutorio Dei nihil agis, nihil boni dico, nam ad male agendum habes sine adjutorio Dei liberam voluntatem: quanquam non est illa libera. *Sermo 156,* 11, 12; t. 38, col. 856." [35]

"Saint Augustin marque toujours soigneusement:
1° *Que les vertus des païens,* bien qu'elles soient des vertus morales réelles, n'ont jamais que l'apparence des vertus chrétiennes; *Dieu les leur* accorde *pour nous inciter* par leur exemple à acquérir les vertus vraies *si elles nous* manquent, et nous détourner de nous en glorifier *si nous les* possédons déjà. *De civ. Dei,* V, 18, 3; t. 41, col. 165. *Ibid.,* V, 19; col. 105-106 [sic].—*Epist. 138,* III, 17; t. 33, col. 533 ... *Epist. 144,* 2; t. 33, col. 591.—*De patientia* XXVII, 28 [sic]; t. 40, col. 624. —*De gratia Christi,* XXIV, 25; t. 44, col. 376 [sic].—*Op. imp. cont. Julian.,* IV, 13, 16; t. 44, col. 744 [sic].
2.° "*Ces vertus naturelles* sont stériles de toute valeur surnatu-

---

[34] A. Camus, *Métaphysique Chrétienne* ..., in *Essais,* p. 1297. The reference "P. L, 18; t. 35: col. 414" should read "P. L., t. 35, col. 1414.
[35] E. Gilson, *op. cit.,* p. 190. The reference "*In Johan.,* V, 1; t. 35, col. 414" should read "... col. 1414." Camus simply copied Gilson's error, (cf. footnote 36).

quaest. 83, 66 P. L, t. 40, col. 63.] L'orgueil est le péché de Satan. Notre *seule fin légitime* au contraire c'est Dieu." [36]

relle. Bien plus, *elles deviennent autant de vices lorsque,* comme il n'est que trop porté à le faire, l'homme s'en attribue le mérite et *s'en glorifie.* La *seule fin légitime est Dieu* . . . Voir *De civitate Dei,* XXI, 16; t. 41, col. 730; et surtout *op. cit.,* XIX, 25, le chapitre intitulé: *Quod non possint ibi verae esse virtutes, ubi non est vera religio;* t. 41, col. 656.—*De div. quaest. 83,* 66, 5; t. 40, col. 63." [37]

"*La Foi est le commencement de la Grâce.*" [38]

"Mais nous venons de voir que *la foi est le commencement de la grâce* . . ." [39]

"*Le dernier aveu de Saint Augustin* sur cette question vitale pour un Chrétien *est un aveu d'ignorance.*" [40]

"Ainsi *le dernier mot d'Augustin* sur cet obscur problème *est un aveu d'ignorance.*" [41]

His analysis of the Pelagian heresy, as well as his summary of Augustine's doctrine of the Word and the Trinity, are taken textually and at random from J. Tixeront's *Histoire des Dogmes.* [42] In some instances, Camus' transcription of his source produces a total misinterpretation of Tixeront's thought. [43] A complete inventory of Camus' borrowings from Tixeront would be as tedious as it is unnecessary. A few examples will suffice to show to what extent Camus' language echoes Tixeront's *History of Christian Dogma*:

---

[36] A. Camus, *Métaphysique Chrétienne* . . ., in *Essais,* p. 1298. The reference "*De gratia Christi,* XXIV, 25, P. L., t. 44. *Id.* 376" should read ". . . t. 44, col. 372."

[37] E. Gilson, *op. cit.,* p. 191, note 1. The reference "*Ibid.,* V, 19; col. 105-106" should read ". . . col. 165-166." Camus evidently noticed Gilson's error, which he proceeded to rectify. — The reference "*De Patientia,* XXVII, 28" should read ". . . XXVII, 35." Here again, Camus rectified Gilson's error. — The reference "*De gratia Christi,* . . . col. 376" should read "*De gratia Christi,* . . . col. 372." In this instance Camus reproduced Gilson's error. — The reference "*Op. imp. cont. Julian.,* IV, 13, 16; t. 44, col. 744" should read "*Contra Iulianum,* IV, 3, 16." Camus dropped this reference.

[38] A. Camus, *Métaphysique Chrétienne* . . ., in *Essais,* p. 1298.

[39] E. Gilson, *op. cit.,* p. 194.

[40] A. Camus, *Métaphysique Chrétienne* . . ., in *Essais,* p. 1298.

[41] E. Gilson, *op. cit.,* p. 197.

A. Camus (*Mét. Chrétienne,* in *Essais,* Paris, 1965.)	J. Tixeront (*Hist. des Dogmes* vol. II, Paris, 1931.)
"*Moine breton, Pélage* craignait au fond une certaine complaisance dans le péché qui peut *se tirer* des doctrines de prédestination . . . Selon Pélage *l'homme a été créé libre. A son gré* il peut *faire le Bien ou le Mal.* Cette liberté *c'est une émancipation de Dieu.* "Libertas arbitrii, qua a Deo emancipatus homo est, in admittendi peccati et abstinendi a peccato possibilitate consistit." [Note 2, bottom of the page: *Julien: ap. Aug. Contra Julianum:* I. 78; P. L., t. 45, col. 1101 [sic]. See also *Pélage: Libellus Fidei* 13.] [44]	"*le moine breton Pélage* supportait qu'avec impatience les excuses que les pécheurs *tiraient* la fragilité de l'homme . . . *L'homme a été créé libre*: cette liberté consiste à pouvoir *à son gré faire ou eviter le mal*: *c'est une émancipation* vis-à-vis *de Dieu,* en vertu de laquelle l'homme s'appartient et se conduit suivant son bon plaisir: "Libertas arbitrii . . . [same quotation] [Note 1, bottom of the page: *Julien ap. August., Contra Iulian. op. imperf.,* I, 78, 79; Pélage, *Libell. fidei,* 13.*"*] [45]

On the Augustinian doctrine of the Trinity:

A. Camus (*Mét. Chrétienne, Essais, Paris,* 1965.)	J. Tixeront, *Hist. des Dogmes,* vol. II, Paris, 1931.)
"Saint Agustin *dans son exposé part du Dieu* [sic], non *comme source des deux autres* essences, *mais de la nature unique* de la Trinité: "Unus quippe deus est ipsa Trinitas et sic unus deus quomodo unus creator. [Note 2, bottom of the page: *Contra Sermon,* 3.]	"*Dans son exposé, il part non du Père comme source des deux autres* personnes, *mais de la nature divine* une et simple qui est *Trinité*: "Unus quippe . . . [same Latin quotation.] De cette unicité et *identité* de nature dans *les trois personnes,* saint Agustin tire les *conséquences* suivantes: 1° Ces

[42] J. Tixeront, *Histoire des dogmes dans l'antiquité chrétienne* (Paris, 1931), vol. II, pp. 354-512.

[43] The reader should compare *Mét. Chrétienne* (*Essais.* pp. 1299-1301 and 1302-04) with J. Tixeront's *Histoire des dogmes,* vol. II, pp. 437-485 and 364-379. The textual resemblances are numerous and striking.

[44] A. Camus, *Métaphysique Chrétienne* . . . , in *Essais,* p. 1299. The reference "*Julien* . . . *Contra Julianum* . . . t. 45, col. 1101" should read ". . . col. 1102." Camus evidently took the trouble of verifying Tixeront's quotation in the P. L.

[45] J. Tixeront, *op. cit.,* II, p. 437-8.

"Les trois personnes sont donc identiques. De là trois *conséquences* fondamentales: les trois personnes n'ont *qu'une seule volonté et une seule opération.* "Ubi nullam [sic] naturam esse, nulla est diuersitas voluntatum." [Note 3, bottom of the page: Contra Maximinum, II 10.] *Ce n'est donc pas le Verbe seul qui est apparu* sur la *terre mais la Trinité tout entière."* *"Dans l'incarnation du Fils, c'est la Trinité tout entière* qui s'unit au corps humain." [Note 4: *De Trinit.* II, 8, 9, P. I, t. 42, col. 85.] [46]

personnes n'ont *ad extra qu'une seule volonté et une seule opération*: "Ubi nulla naturarum nulla est diversitas voluntatum;" [Note 7, bottom of the page: *Contra Maximinum*, II, 10, 2; *De Trinit.* II, 9; *Enchiridion*, XXXVIII] et le saint docteur en prend occasion de réformer la théorie des théophanies présentée par ses devanciers. *Ce n'est pas le Verbe seul qui a apparu, mais toute la Trinité,* mais Dieu... *Dans l'Incarnation du Fils,* l'acte qui a uni le Fils avec la nature humaine et qui l'a ainsi envoyé dans le monde est *le fait de toute la Trinité."* [Note 2, bottom of the page: *De trinit.,* II, 8, 9.] [47]

The latter example demonstrates that Camus' misinterpretation of the Augustinian teaching on the Trinity is due to a transcription of several passages in J. Tixeront's *Histoire des Dogmes* taken out of context. Whereas Augustine asserted that, in the Old Testament theophanies, the Trinity as a whole had appeared to mankind, Camus interprets Tixeront as stating that Augustine held to the Incarnation not only of the Son, *but of the entire Trinity.* Camus' misreading of such a basic point gives some idea of the haste with which he must have been working.

Part three of Camus' analysis is, on the whole, a *réchauffé* of Etienne Gilson's *Introduction to a Study of Saint Augustine.* [48] In some cases, Camus acknowledges his debt to Gilson, while in others, he avoids doing so. [49] The text "Si non potes intelligere... crede ut intelligas," which Camus allegedly discovered in Augustine's *In Johan-*

---

[46] A. Camus, *Métaphysique Chrétienne* ..., in *Essais,* p. 1303.

[47] J. Tixeront, *op. cit.,* II, pp. 364-5.

[48] A. Camus, *Métaphysique Chrétienne* ..., in *Essais,* pp. 1304-1306; cf. E. Gilson, *op. cit.,* pp. 31-43, and p. 293.

[49] For example, A. Camus, *Métaphysique Chrétienne...* in *Essais,* p. 1305: "La vraie philosophie débute par un acte d'adhésion à l'ordre surnaturel, qui libéra la volonté de la chair par la grâce et la pensée du scepticisme par la révélation." (The text is taken from Gilson, *op. cit.,* p. 294: "libéra" should read "libère.")

nis Tractatum, is in fact a contradiction of two separate quotations taken from one of Gilson's footnotes. [50] As for the sentence "Ce n'est pas à Dieu qu'il faut croire, mais en Dieu," it is copied out of Gilson. [51] It would be excessive to pretend that the entire chapter on Augustine is plagiarized. Some of the work is unequivocally Camus' own. He can, in fact, be criticized for giving personal solutions to certain problems which he would have approached more reservedly had a wider acquaintance with the sources enabled him to realize their complexity. For example, what Camus calls the "famous passage," in Book VII of the *Confessions* ("I read . . . that the Word was from the beginning, that the Word was in God and that the Word was God . . . But I did not read that the Word was made Man and dwelt among us . . . ."), clarifies, in his view, the problem of the Neoplatonic elements in Augustine's thinking. "Contrasting Incarnation to Contemplation, Saint Augustine immediately crystallized the oppositions and the resemblances between the two systems of thought." [52] Camus thus seems to assume that the parallel between the Prologue of Saint John and the Neoplatonic writings leapt to Augustine's mind the very moment he read the *libri platonici*. [53] He forgets the elementary fact that the "famous passage" of Book VII was written around 398, more than ten years after Augustine's first encounter with Neoplatonic writings, and that it was presumably sometime after this first encounter with the Neoplatonic writings that Camus became conscious of their resemblance to St. John's Prologue. Despite his allusion to P. Alfaric's "excessive conclusions" on the subject of Neoplatonic influences, Camus is evidently unacquainted with the complexity of the subject he raises. [54]

The general summary and conclusion of chapter four is also, presumably, Camus' own:

---

[50] A. Camus, *Ibid.,* p. 1305. The "two quotations in question are to be found on p. 33: "Si non potes intelligere, crede ut intelligas; præcedit fides, sequitur intellectus." *Sermo* 118, 1; t. 38, col. 672. —"Ergo noli quærere intelligere ut credas, sed crede ut intelligas". *In Joan. Tract.* 29, 6; t. 35, c. 1630. Camus contracted them into a single quotation.

[51] E. Gilson, *Ibid.,* p. 36.

[52] A. Camus, *Métaphysique Chrétienne . . . ,* in *Essais,* p. 1294. Camus' reference to "*Confessions,* VIII, C, IX," should read *Conf.,* VII, 9, 13-14.

[53] *Ibid:* "Augustin a fixé du premier coup les oppositions et les ressemblances des deux pensées."

[54] *Ibid.* For these "conclusions excessives," see P. Alfaric, *op. cit.,* pp. 374-376; and E. Portalié, art "Augustin (saint)." *Dict. de Th. Catch.,* col. 2325.

Augustinism marks both an end and a beginning. We have indicated what path evangelical Christianity had to follow in order to reach this point. The capital fact of this evolution was its break with Judaism and its appearance in the Graeco-Roman world. From that moment on, the fusion began to take place. Prepared by the Oriental religions, Mediterranean thought prepared itself to be fertilized by this new civilization. Neoplatonism can be considered as the catalyst of this fertilization, because it, too, was the product of the same Graeco-Oriental syncretism. The dogmatic formulas of Christianity were a combination of that syncretism and the essential premises of Evangelical faith. [55]

This conclusion is as irrefutable as it is banal. Camus is here summarizing general ideas with which any historian of the Patristic era would have to agree. As for his final remarks of the important influence of Augustinian thought on the Middle Ages, no one could possibly take issue with them. [56]

* * *

The breadth of Camus' subject forced him to work with speed. Since he evidently did not have the time to read Augustine's original works, he was reduced to a direct utilization of secondary sources. In itself, this procedure is quite acceptable, and in the preparation of a student thesis, it can even be necessary. Camus can, however, be taken to task for having summarized, or plagiarized, his secondary sources, while his footnote references give the illusory impression that his work is the product of original research.

Camus should not be judged with undue severity for the sort of scholarly tactics at which most university students, at one time or other, have tried their hand. It would be foolish to pretend that *Christian Metaphysics* is a major literary work, or that its poor scholarly value in any way diminishes the quality of Camus' mature production. Camus' chapter on Augustine did, however, lay the foundations for several of his later indictments against Augustinism and Christianity, and it served as a reference in the preparation of some

---

[55] *Ibid.*, p. 1306.

[56] It would be particularly interesting to compare Camus' general conclusions with those of Portalié's aricle, *op. cit.*, col. 2319-2321, *"De quelle nature est l'influence d'Augustin."*

of his later works. While *Christian Metaphysics* cannot be considered as a major work, Camus himself seems to have attached a certain amount of importance to it. A remark, in his *Carnets,* would lead one to believe, in fact, that he had perhaps intended to revise and publish *Christian Metaphysics.* [57] But whatever the reasons, Camus never did revise his essay. His first prolonged contact with Augustine, in 1936, was undoubtedly his last, and his first impressions, however superficial, even occasionally erroneous, were never to be corrected, modified, or renewed.

II. *Later Works*

In his later works, Camus makes both implicit and explicit references to Augustine's person and to Augustinian themes and ideas. One wonders whether an implicit reference to Augustine is not to be found in *Noces à Tipasa,* from Camus' early collection of essays entitled *Noces.* As he proclaims his mystical, pagan love for the earth, sea, and sky of North Africa, the author exclaims: We have so often been told about pride.... You know, it is the Sin of Satan.... But at other moments I cannot prevent myself from proclaiming a pride in living which the whole world conspires to give me. At Tipasa, 'I see' is equivalent to 'I believe.' " [58]

Roger Quilliot, a distinguished editor and critic of Camus' work, believes the last sentence to be a "profane transposition" of an alleged "Augustinian formula," "I would not believe if I did not see that it is necessary to believe." [59] Since Quilliot does not specify the source of this "Augustinian formula," it is impossible to know exactly which text of Augustine's he might be referring to to. The formula might well be a transposition of the famous "crede ut intelligas."

It seems likely, however, that in writing *Noces à Tipasa,* Camus intended to bring up some of the important themes of his essay on Christian Metaphysics with which *Noces* is contemporaneous. One of the sentences from *Noces à Tipasa,* for example, is a verbatim transcription of a sentence from the "diplôme:" "At the mysteries of

---

[57] A. Camus, *Carnets* (Paris, 1964), vol. II, p. 342: "Reprendre le passage de l'Héllenisme au Christianisme, véritable et seul tournant de l'histoire."

[58] A. Camus, *Noces à Tipasa,* in *Essais,* p. 59.

[59] A. Camus, *Essais,* p. 1348 ("Notes et Variantes").

Eleusis, all one needed to do was contemplate." [60] In its context, in
Christian Metaphysics, Camus is thus describing the basic distinction
between the Greek idea that understanding suffices as an initiation
to the divine mysteries and the Christian idea that "one can believe
in God and yet not be saved." [61] Camus' deliberate equation of seeing
and understanding with belief, in *Noces à Tipasa,* translates his need
for a Greek religious initiation. Whoever does not believe in tran-
scendental forms of religion, in short, finds the distinction between
understanding and belief to be meaningless. Camus is thus professing
his Hellenic faith, and implicitly rejecting the Christian (and Augustinian) teaching that initiation to the Christian faith through baptism
does not necessarily entail salvation. [62]

One of Camus' most passionate if implicit diatribes against Augustinian Christianity occurred during a talk a group of Dominicans at
the convent of Latour-Maubourg in 1946. Camus had previously been
annoyed by accusations from Christian and Marxist circles that his
thinking was "pessimistic." And he took advantage of this occasion
to remind his listeners, most of them Christians, of two of the most
somber themes of Augustinian theology: that of man's universal misery
without Grace, and that of the damnation of unbaptized children. Without explicitly mentioning Augustine, he exclaimed: "Moreover, what
right has a Christian or a Marxist to accuse me of pessimism? It is
not I who invented the 'misery of the creature,' nor the terrifying
formulas of divine malediction. It is not I who exclaimed 'Nemo
bonus,' nor I who preached the damnation of unbaptized children. It
is not I who said that man was incapable of saving himself by his
own power, and that from the depths of his misery his only hope was
in the grace of God." [63] Camus considerd Jesus' words, "nemo bonus
nisi unus Deus" (as recorded by Mark), as a perfect summary of
Christian pessimism towards the human condition. [64] The "Nemo
bonus" must have been a particularly obsessive theme during that
period, for several weeks before his talk to the Dominicans, Camus

---

[60] A. Camus, *Noces à Tipasa,* in *Essais,* p. 57; cf. *Métaphysique chrétienne, Essais,* p. 1252.
[61] *Ibid.,* p. 1252.
[62] *Ibid.*
[63] A. Camus, *L'Incroyant et les Chrétiens,* in *Essais,* pp. 373-4.
[64] *Mark X:* 18: "Quid me dicis bonum? Nemo bonus, nisi unus Deus."

had recorded the following reflections in his *Carnets*: "The only great Christian mind to look the problem of evil in the face was Saint Augustine. His conclusion was the terrifying 'nemo bonus.' Since then, Christianity has spent its time giving the problem temporary solutions

"The result is there for everyone to see. It took time, but men have become intoxicated with a poison that dates back two thousand years. They have had enough of evil, or they are resigned to it, which is pretty much the same thing. But at least they can no longer put up with lies on that subject." [65]

Ten years earlier, in *Christian Metaphysics*, Camus had equated the "nemo bonus" of Mark with the pessimism of Paul and Augustine:

> In sin, man becomes conscious of his misery and his pride. "Nemo bonus" [Note: Mark X, 18] "Omnes peccaverunt." [Note: Romans III, 23]. Sin is universal. But of all the significant texts of the New Testament, few are as rich in meaning and penetration as this passage from the Epistle to the Romans [Note: VII, 15-24]: "I cannot understand my actions. I fail to perform the good thins to which I aspire, and I commit the evil things that I loathe. If I do those things that I do not want to do, then it is not I that do them, but sin, which resides in me. When I want to do good, I discover that a fatal law has placed evil within me. The interior man in me is happy with God's law, but I feel within every part of my body another law which fights against the law of the spirit, and which enslaves me to the law of sin that is in my body." [66]

These New Testament texts were direct anticipations of Augustine's pessimism: "Here, Augustine's 'non posse non peccare' begins to take shape. The pessimistic Christian attitude towards the world begins to develop. This attitude and these aspirations are answered by the constructive part of evangelical Christianity." [67]

In point of fact, although Camus was correct in linking the "pessimism" of Saint Paul with that of Saint Augustine, he was wrong in his interpretation of the "nemo bonus," and invariably quoted these words out of context. In mark X, 18 (Vulgate), Jesus answers one

---

[65] A. Camus, *Carnets*, II. p. 179 (October, 1946).
[66] A. Camus, *Métaphysique Chrétienne . . .*, in *Essais*, p. 1234-5.
[67] *Ibid.*, p. 1235.

of his disciples, who has called him "bonus," by saying: "Quid me dicis bonus? Nemo bonus, nisi unus Deus." Far from underscoring man's ignominy, Jesus is saying that *bonus,* in its full sense, is a word that can be applied only to God. (Augustine, incidentally, systematically commented the passage in this sense, and never thought of linking it to his doctrine of "non posse non peccare," i.e. man's "incapacity not to sin," which, according to him, is a result of the fall of Man.) [68]

As for the "damnation" of unbaptized children, it seems to have stood out, in Camus' mind, as one of the essential and most terrifying of Augustine's doctrines. [69] Camus, one remembers, had stated, in *Christian Metaphysics,* that the "logical consequence" of Augustine's doctrine of grace was that all humanity, but for God's mercy, was damned to hell, including unbaptized children: "We depend upon divine grace. Damnation is theoretically universal. The entire human race is doomed to the everlasting fire. Its only hope is in the mercy of God. It follows that unbaptized children are also damned." [70]

It should be pointed out that Augustine's "doctrine" on the fate of unbaptized children is neither as dogmatic nor as horrifying as Camus somewhat morbidly enjoyed making it. In response to Pelagius' assertion that man was capable of achieving salvation by himself, Augustine held that the supernatural vision was impossible without Grace. [71] On this point, Augustine was merely being faithful to the mainstream of Christian teaching since St. Paul. What, then, became of unbaptized children? St. Augustine seems to have been as tortured by the human aspect of the problem as was Camus fifteen centuries later. In an early work, Augustine had proposed a hypothetical "intermediate state" between Hell and Heaven, wherein unbaptized children would dwell. He later retracted this position and concluded that unbaptized children would be subjected to the mildest form of punishment, "poena

---

[68] For example, see Augustine, *Contra Sermones Arian.,* cap. 35, P. L. XLII, col. 707.

[69] Camus, summary of the Augustinian "doctrine" on the damnation of unbaptized children is a somewhat haphazard recapitulation of J. Tixeront, *op. cit.,* II, pp. 480-481.

In the spring of 1968, I received a latter from Brice Parain, a friend of Camus' at the "Editions Gallimard," in which he said that "Camus was *indignant* that Saint Augustine should send children to hell."

[70] A. Camus, *Métaphysique Chrétienne . . . ,* in *Essais,* p. 1301.

[71] J. Tixeront, *op. cit.,* II, p. 481.

mitissima." [72] Far from ending the debate, Augustine had merely launched it. By the thirteenth century, the theory of damnation had been abandoned, and the hypothesis of an intermediate state had become the most widely-held theological position. [73] The Thomistic doctrine of limbo is a position still currently accepted by many Catholic theologians, but the problem, by its very nature, and because of the paucity of Scriptural information on which any eventual "solution" can be based, still preoccupies theologians in their idle hours. [74]

It would not be fair to say that Camus misinterpreted Augustine's position, since Augustine *did* hold to a *poena mitissima*. Unlike J. Tixeront (his main source), Camus gave the impression that Augustine's teaching was brutal, unqualified, and authoritarian, and that it represented a teaching from which Christian theology had never deviated: a somewhat unflattering illustration of the extent to which Christianity, in Camus' mind, coincided with "Augustinism."

* * *

The Plague, which appeared in 1947, was intended to be, by Camus' own admission, the most "anti-Christian" of his works. Is it, therefore, the most anti-Augustinian? Without doing one's imagination an undue violence, one might consider Paneloux as a latter-day version of the bishop of Hippo. The problem, in any case, deserves critical attention.

The plague has been raging at Oran for several weeks when Father Paneloux, the Jesuit priest, decides to write a "vehement sermon" on the moral consequences that can be drawn from this sinister event. [75] The narrator remarks that, in order to find time to prepare his sermon, Paneloux "desisted from the research work on Saint Augustine and the African Church, that had won for him a high place in his Order." [76] Fresh from his Augustinian research, does it not seem logical

---

[72] F. Cayré, "Une Rétractation de Saint Augustin," in *L'Année Théologique Augustienne*, 1952, II, p. 136.

[73] *Ibid.*, p. 140.

[74] See, for example, C. Journet, *La Volonté Divine Salvifique sur les Petits Enfants* (Paris, 1958), p. 151; also pp. 183-185 and passim.

[75] A. Camus, *La Peste*, in *Théâtre, Récits, Nouvelles d'Albert Camus* (Paris, 1962), p. 1292.

[76] A. Camus, *The Plague*, translated by Stuart Gilbert (New York, 1948), p. 85. Unless otherwise indicated, all quotations from *The Plague* are taken from Mr. Gilbert's translation.

that Paneloux' sermon should be in keeping with Augustinian thought or retain some resonance of it? (In an earlier draft of the novel, Camus had written that Paneloux "had published commentaries on Augustine which showed him to be *entirely* converted to his Master's doctrine." [77] One should immediately specify, however, that Camus' Paneloux is not just an ordinary "Augustinian," but a Jesuit Augustinian — which is supposed to mean (one presumes) that he is capable of adapting his Augustinism to any circumstance. A Jesuit who directs a parish in North Africa and writes books on Augustine and the African Church is bound to be a versatile, if somewhat overworked, ecclesiastic.

In his first sermon, Paneloux tells his brethren exactly what they have come to hear: "Calamity has come on you, my brethren, and, my brethren, you have deserved it." [78] The main ideas can be summarized as follows: the people of Oran are suffering; God often sends such calamities to humiliate the arrogant and the blind of heart; the people of Oran have sinned and compromised with evil; in visiting them with affliction, God is showing his mercy, for the plague is both a calamity and a means of finding one's way back to Him.

The first sermon does not seem to contain a single explicit Augustinian formula. It is, however, fiilled with "thematic echoes" of Augustine's works; and Paneloux' theological vision of evil, once pruned of its rhetoric, seems particularly Augustinian.

Faithful to what one assumes to be "his master's doctrine," Paneloux does not for a moment pretend that the plague is a substantial or ontological evil. He rather chooses to sidestep any classification of the event, and to dwell upon its moral antecedents and consequences. At the source of all human suffering is man's sin, or, to put it in Augustinian terms: "Sin is the cause. We have sinned through one man, and all of us have been born into corruption. The cause of all our misery is sin. Men do not suffer evil without reason. God is just. God is all-powerful. We should not suffer these things, if we did not deserve them." [79]

---

[77] A. Camus, *Notes et Variantes de la Peste*, in *Théâtre . . .* , p. 1979.

[78] A. Camus, *The Plague* (Gilbert translation), pp. 86-87.

[79] St. Augustine, *Sermo CCXL*, cap. 3, P. L. XXXVIII, col. 1131: "Causa peccatum est. In uno peccauimus, et omnes ad corruptionem nati sumus. Malorum omnium nostrorum causa peccatum est. Non enim sine causa hominis mala patiuntur. Iustus est Deus, omnipotens est Deus: nullo modo ista pateremur, si non mereremur.

"This calamity", according to Paneloux, "was not willed by God." [80] It is one of Augustine's most common assertions that God is not the "author" of evil: "Let it be understood by those who can understand that God is not the author of evil. How, in fact, can God, who is responsible for the existence of all things, also be responsible for their non-existence, that is, for their deviation from their essence and their inclination towards non-being?" [81]

Several of Paneloux' other statements cannot fail to recall Augustinian themes, not to say Augustinian phrases. "Too long," he says, "this world of ours has connived at evil, too long it has counted on the divine mercy ..." [82] ["Let no one," says Augustine, "count too heavily on God's mercy."] [33] "For a long while God gazed down on this town with eyes of compassion; but He grew weary of waiting, His eternal hope was too long deferred, and now He has turned His face away from us .... And thus, my brothers, at last it is revealed to you, the divine compassion which has ordained good and evil in everything .... [84] ["Therefore, even when the Lord visits us or allows us to be visited with affliction, even then is He merciful .... When my tribulation rises to a certain degree of suffering, Lord, let your Mercy intervene to turn it to good ends."] [85] "This same pestilence which is slaying you works for your good and points your path." [86] ["He is most merciful not to leave our iniquities unpunished. He deigns to flail us moderately, so as not to be compelled to damn us to the deepest hell."] [87]

---

[80] A. Camus, *The Plague*, p. 87.

[81] St. Augustine, *De Moribus Manichæorum*, Lib. II, P. L. XXXII, col. 1346: "... intelligitur ab eis qui hoc possunt intelligere, non esse Deum auctorem mali. Quomodo enim potest ille, qui omnium quæ sunt, eausa est ut sint, causa esse rursus ut non sint, id est, ut ab essentia deficiant et ad non esse tendant?"

[82] A. Camus, *The Plague*, p. 88.

[83] St. Augustine, *Enarratio in Psalmum XLIV*, P. L. XXXVI, col. 505: "Nemo sibi multum de misericordia Dei blandiatur."

[84] A. Camus, *The Plague*, pp. 88-90.

[85] St. Augustine, *Enarratio in Psalmum XLIV*, P. L. XXXVI, col. 854-5: "Ergo et quando Dominus permittit aut facit ut in tribulatione aliqua simus ..."

[86] A. Camus, *The Plague*, p. 90.

[87] St. Augustine, *Sermo CLXXI*, cap. 4, P. L., XXXVIII, col. 934-5.

Paneloux ends his sermon with a historical anecdote: "Many centuries ago the Christians of Abyssinia saw in the plague a sure and God-sent means of winning eternal life. Those who were not yet stricken wrapped round them sheets in which men had died of the plague, so as to make sure of their death. I grant you such a frenzied quest of salvation was not to be commended.... No man should seek to force God's hand or to hurry on the appointed hour.... Yet we can learn a salutary lesson from the zeal, excessive though it was, of the Abyssinian Christians. [88] Though this historical anecdote was taken from another source, it could easily have been imagined by Augustine. [89] In the *City of God,* Augustine brings up, in theoretical terms, a moral problem much like the one posed in anecdotal terms by Paneloux. Is it licit, asks Augustine, for a Christian virgin to kill herself voluntarily, so as to avoid dishonor? To his own question, Augustine, like Paneloux, replies that, though such zeal may seem commendable, "no one should hurry on the appointed hour." "Whoever kills himself is a homicide; and he is as guilty in killing himself as he was innocent of the cause that drove him to kill himself." [90] For, Augustine continues, if the suicide of a traitor like Judas is detestable, how much more detestable is the suicide of an innocent man. To commit suicide out of religious devotion, therefore, remains an illicit, if understandable, impulse. [91]

Paneloux' first sermon ends on as Augustinian note: "It [that radiant, eternal light which glows ... in the dark core of suffering] reveals the will of God in action, unfailingly transforming evil into good." [92] One cannot help being reminded of a key Augustinian phrase,

---

[88] A. Camus, *The Plague,* p. 90.

[89] Camus had taken this anecdote from a work entitled *Défense de l'Europe contre la Peste,* Masson, 1897 (according to R. Quilliot, *Notes à "La Peste,"* in A. Camus, *Théâtre* ... p. 1980).

[90] St. Augustine, *De Civ. Dei,* I cap. xvii, P. L., XLI, col. 30-31: "qui se autem occidit, homicida est; et tanto fit nocentior, cum se occiderit, quanto innocentior in ea causa fuit, qua se occidendum putavit."

[91] *Ibid.;* "Cur autem homo, qui mali nihil fecit, sibi male faciat, et se ipsum interficiendo hominem interficiat innocentem, ne alium patiatur nocentem; atque in se perpetret peccatum proprium, ne in eo perpetretur alienum."

[92] A. Camus, *The Plague,* p. 90.

which recurs in varying forms throughout his work: "Deus malis uti bene nouit — God knows the good use that can be made of evil." [93]

As to Paneloux' final recommendation, that "our fellow citizens would ofer up to heaven that one prayer which is truly Christian, a prayer of love . . . . And God would see to the rest . . . . ," [94] does it not echo the meaning and the rhythm of Augustine's celebrated formula: "Digile Deum, et quod vis fac"? [95]

A personal crisis separates the second sermon from the first. After witnessing the agony and death of the stricken child, Paneloux "seemed changed." His assurance is shaken, not to mention his faith. Each of his attempts to understand the logic of divine justice makes him less sure of himself than before. How can one explain, how can one justify the agony of this innocent child? Faced with this question, which is rather an indictment than a query, Paneloux' philosophical system crumbles. It is a different man who mounts slowly into the pulpit to deliver his second sermon. This time his listeners are few, and they immediately notice that he no longer addresses them as "you," but as "we." The indirect style of the narration underscores what the narrator describes as the "gentler, more thoughtful tone than on the previous occasion:" [96]

> What he, Father Paneloux, had said in his first sermon still held good — such, anyhow, was his belief . . . there were some things we could grasp as touching God, and others we could not. There was no doubt as to the existence of good and evil and, as a rule, it was easy to see the difference between them. The difficulty began when we looked into the nature of evil, and among things evil he included human suffering. Thus we had apparently needful pain, and apparently needless pain . . . he might easily have assured them that the child's sufferings would be compensated for by an eternity of bliss awaiting him. But how could he give that

---

[93] E. G., *De Civ. Dei*, XIV, cap. xxvii, P. L., XLI, col. 435: "Quoniam qui providenter atque omnipotenter sua cuique distribuit, non solum bonis, uerum etiam malis bene uti nouit." Cf. *Contra Iulianum*, cap. lx, P. L., XLV, col. 1495: "Deus tamen tam bonus est, ut malis quoque utatur bene, quae Omnipotens esse non sineret, si eis bene uti summa sua bonitate non posset . . . . "

[94] A. Camus, *The Plague*, p. 91.

[95] St. Augustine, *In Epist. Ioannis*, tract. VIII, 8, P. L. XXXV, col. 2033.

[96] A. Camus, *The Plague*, p. 200.

assurance when, to tell the truth, he knew nothing about it? For who would dare to assert that eternal happiness can compensate for a single moment's human suffering? He who asserted that would not be a true Christian, a follower of the Master who knew all the pangs of suffering in his body and his soul .... "My brothers ... we must believe everything or deny everything .... "

....

"My brothers" — the preacher's tone showed he was nearing the conclusion of his sermon — "the love of God is a hard love It demands total self-surrender, disdain of our human personality. And yet it alone can reconcile us to suffering and the deaths of children, it alone can justify them, since we cannot understand them .... " [97]

It would be wrong to consider the second sermon as a repudiation of the first. Paradoxically enough, though it is more "existential" in tone, it also tends to be more academic in spots, and more abstract ("the difficulty began when we looked into the nature of evil"). From an Augustinian point of view, two points immediately stand out as un-Augustinian: Paneloux now considers the plague as a substantial or ontological evil ("and among things evil he included human suffering"); and, though he believes in the existence of a transcendent truth, he no longer believes in the ability of human reason to attain that truth. Paneloux, therefore, denies the Augustinian contention (inherited from Plotinus and the Neoplatonists) that the essence of evil is "wholly negative," and unsubstantial; and he strays from the Augustinian position on the relation of Faith to Reason. What Paneloux is now suggesting is not the classical Augustinian thesis that Faith is the key to rational comprehension — "crede ut intelligas" — but that comprehension is simply impossible — "crede, quia non potes intelligere." What Camus had referred to as the Augustinian "compromise" between Faith and Reason is broken, and it is Reason that is defeated. Indeed, the most striking feature of the second sermon is anti-rationalism, coupled with fideism: "there were some things we could grasp ... and others not ... he knew nothing about it ... who would dare assert ... ? ... we must believe everything or deny everything ... we cannot understand .... "

---

[97] *Ibid.*, pp. 200-205.

Was the second sermon intended to represent a break with Christianity? or a mere break with Augustinian teaching? It is impossible to tell what the artist's intentions were. During the second sermon, it crosses Rieux's mind that Paneloux is "dallying with heresy," and a young deacon who has been following the evolution of Paneloux' views is openly worried about the audacity of his thinking. [98] In point of fact, the second sermon has nothing heretical about it; nor is it entirely "liberated" of its Augustinian influences. The language of the second sermon is sometimes more Augustinian than that of the first. For example, Paneloux' peroration, "the love of God is a hard love ... it demands ... disdain of our human personality," is almost a literal translation of Augustine's description of "celestial love" in *The City of God*: "terrenam [amorem] scilicet amor sui usque ad contemptum Dei, cœlestem a[morem] uero amor Dei usque ad contemptum sui." [99] And Paneloux' distinction between "needful" and "needless" pain is somewhat reminiscent of Camus' distinction between "natural" and "moral" evil in Augustine. [100] The second sermon cannot, therefore, be interpreted as a complete repudiation of Augustinism, as Augustine could have written parts of it himself.

It is safe to assume, however, that Paneloux, though he does not explicitly refute the Augustinian theology of evil, no longer finds it viable. Could Augustine have "included" human suffering among things evil, while remaining faithful to his Neoplatonic convictions? Would Augustine have denied the capacity of reason (enlightened by faith) to understand and explain suffering? Would Augustine have been so fideistic as to declare "we must believe everything or deny everything"? Such a pathetic cry has too modern a ring about it to be Augustinian. A Christian who describes his faith in terms of an absolute alternative has been reading more of Kierkegaard than of Augustine.

What of the specific problem about which the entire second sermon turns, that of suffering children? Surely, long before Dostoyevsky, Augustine had realized that the agony and death of children seems to constitute the most unanswerable argument against divine justice. In the *De libero arbitrio* he poses the problem of the suffering and

---

[98] *Ibid.*, pp. 202 and 206.
[99] *De Civ. Dei*, XIV, chapter 28, in P. L., XLI, col. 436.
[100] A. Camus, *Métaphysique Chrétienne* ..., in *Essais*, p. 1295.

death of children, in order to reply to what he calls "the complaint of the inexperienced" (*"imperitorum querela"*). "There are those," says Augustine, "who ask: 'For what purpose do children suffer and die? Why were they born, if it was only to die before taking advantage of life? How can God judge them if they have committed neither good nor evil?' It must be answered that God can create nothing in vain, neither a man nor a leaf, and that it does not behoove us to fear that there might be no middle way between virtue and sin, or no middle judgment between reward and punishment." [101]

"A graver, and, as it were, more seemingly compassionate complaint (maior querela et quasi misericors) is sometimes brought up, namely, 'why does God allow children to suffer?' 'What harm did they do to suffer thus?' As if innocence were praiseworthy before man acquires the capacity to do evil! Doesn't God amend adults by allowing the suffering and death of the little ones who are so dear to them? If these sufferings offer the parents an incentive to mend their ways, why shouldn't they occur? If the parents did not suffer thus on earth, they would have no way of avoiding punishment at the time of their judgment. Who knows, finally, whether God is not reserving for these little ones a reward that as infinitely superior to their agony!" [102]

This is the very text that Camus seems to be anticipating when he says: "Thus he might easily have assured them that the child's sufferings would be compensated for by an eternity of bliss awaiting him. But how could he give that assurance when, to tell the truth, he knew nothing about it? For who would dare to assert that eternal happiness can compensate for a single moment's human suffering?" [103] Augustine's thesis is here rejected in the very language in which it was presented.

Paneloux deliberately refuses to adopt Augustine's solution to the problem of the suffering of children. It is presumably to underscore the humiliation of his own reason that he decides, once stricken

[101] St. Augustine, *De Libero Arbitrio*, III, cap. xxiii, P. L. **XXXII**, col. 1303-1304.

[102] *Ibid.*: "Quis autem nouit quid paruulis, de quorum cruciatibus duritia maiorum contunditur, aut exercetur fides, aut misericordia probatur; quis ergo nouit quid ipsis paruulis in secreto iudiciorum suorum bonæ compensationis reservet Deus, qui quanquam nihil recte fecerint, tamen nec peccantes aliquid ista perpessi sunt?"

[103] A. Camus, *The Plague*, p. 202.

with the plague, not to resist this unfathomable display of divine will.
Faced with the spectacle of innocent suffering, any reasoning seems to
him as pretentious as it is vain. Desirous of remaining lucid in the
presence of absurdity, this Christian Sisyphus faces death without
resistance, having sacrificed his need to understand in order to remain
faithful to an obscure but personal conception of Christianity. Paneloux
has *silenced* the metaphysician so that the Christian might live. This
once dogmatic disciple of Augustine has realized that a theological
system can be the worst enemy of faith.

* * *

The name of Augustine continues to appear after *The Plague*. In
an interview published in the *Revue du Caire* in 1948, Emile Simon,
a journalist, asked Camus about his attitude towards Christianity. Isn't
the Christian's act of faith, "this submission of reason to the most
scandalous injustice," to be considered as "a resignation and an
escape"? Camus' answer reveals both a singular nobility of mind, and
an unstinting admiration for Augustine: "The insurmountable obstacle
does seems to me to be the problem of evil . . . . But I should think
twice before saying, as you did, that Christian faith is a resignation.
Does this word adequately describe a Saint Augustine or a Pascal?
Honesty requires one to judge a doctrine by its summits, not by its
by-products. Moreover, although I am inexperienced in these matters,
it seems to me that faith is less of a serenity than a tragic hope." [104]

There is also a curious passage in *The Rebel* (part of which has
already been discussed in the previous chapter), wherein Camus con-
trasts Gnosticism with Augustinism:

> It [Gnosticism] also wished to avoid Augustinism in advance,
> insofar as the latter system provides arguments against all
> forms of revolt. For Basilides, for example, the martyrs have
> sinned, as has Christ himself, since they have suffered . . . .
> For an all powerful and arbitrary Grace, the Gnostics ende-
> avored to substitute the Greek notion of initiation, which
> allows man to retain his prerogatives. The wide number of
> Gnostic sects of the "second generation" testifies to the
> wide-ranging effort made by Greek thought to render

---

[104] A. Camus, *Actuelles I*, in *Essais*, p. 380.

the Christian world more accessible, and to disarm metaphysical revolt, which Hellenism considered as the worst possible evil. But the Church condemned this effort, and in so doing, it allowed the rebels to multiply. [105]

This somewhat abstruse passage can more easily be understood in the light of *Christian Metaphysics and Neoplatonism* (particularly chapters two and four). [106] Augustine's stern anti-Pelagian (thereby anti-humanistic) conception of Grace, Camus is suggesting, gave added if involuntary impetus to the movement of metaphysical rebellion, which, in Western culture, is contemporaneous with the personal, voluntaristic God of Judaism and Christianity. Gnosticism represents an abortive attempt to Hellenize Christianity, to explain human suffering in rational terms, and to free the Christian God of any responsibility for evil. Gnosticism, therefore, wished to provide arguments against metaphysical revolt, and, as it were, to steal Augustine's fire. Camus' suggestion that Gnosticism "wished to avoid Augustinism in advance" is provocative, but untenable, unless he can explain how one ideology can "avoid" another that is historically posterior.

* * *

Christian Metaphysics and Neoplatonism can reasonably be considered as a first draft of Camus' attempt to study the problem of evil and revolt in historical terms. Towards the end of Pagan Antiquity, Camus asserts, there arose in Western thought a progressive "softening" of the Hellenic spirit, which tended to conciliate Western man with the cosmic powers rather than widen the abyss between them. If the Incarnation of Christ represents the historical beginning of this conciliation of God and man, Augustine certainly represents its culmination. Augustine determined the course that Western metaphysics was to take for well over a thousand years. Rather than aggravate man's instinctive tendency to revolt against God, Augustinian theology provided intelligible solutions to the very problems that might have triggered revolt. In conciliating Faith with Reason, Augustine checked

---

[105] A. Camus, *L'Homme Révolté*, in *Essais*, p. 443-4.
[106] A. Camus, *Métaphysique Chrétienne...*, in *Essais*, pp. 1250-69 and pp. 1293-1309.

a revolutionary movement whose forebears were Prometheus, Cain, Lucretius, and Epicurus.

Chapter four of *Christian Metaphysics* is Camus' only study of Augustinian literature. In the rest of his work, Augustine makes transitory appearances, and his doctrine is alluded to whenever Camus refers to problems such as evil, grace, human suffering, the "damnation" of unbaptized children, or the modern parallels between Christianity and Marxism. It is doubtful whether Camus pursued any serious reading of Augustine after his student thesis. From his readings as a student he gathered, at best, a certain veneer of Augustinian culture, a general knowledge of several important Augustinian works, usually derived form secondary sources.

Had he read the text of any Augustinian works? In the bibliography which he appended to *Christian Metaphysics,* he claimed to have "consulted" the following texts: *Confessions, De Ciuitate Dei, De Beata Vita, De duabus animis contra Manichæos, Contra Iulianum, De Natura et Gratia, De gestis Pelagii, De gratia Christi et peccati originali, De gratia et libero arbitrio,* as well as some of Augustine's letters and sermons. [107] In point of fact, this list is subject to the strictest caution. Nearly all of Camus' references to the "original texts" were found in secondary sources and uncritically copied. He had, however, probably read parts or all of the *Confessions* in a French translation. [108]

What is the scholarly value of his analysis of Augustinian doctrine? By and large, it is a hasty compilation of his sources, but its very lack of originality makes it generally accurate, with some exceptions. I have dwelt elsewhere with Camus' "method," and need not belabor this point. It is significant that he dwells persistently on what he considers the harsh features of Augustine's works. He is particularly fascinated by Augustine's vision of the universal ravages wrought by original sin; by the absence, within the Augustinian framework, of human autonomy (except the power to sin); by the "conflicting" features of Augustine's doctrine (Grace vs. Freedom, Reason vs. Faith).

---

[107] A. Camus, *Métaphysique Chrétienne...*, in *Essais*, pp. 1312-13.

[108] He seems to have made use of an undated translation of the *Confessions* by Arnauld d'Andilly. Compare the text of Book VII of the *Confessions* quoted by Camus (*Métaphysique Chrétienne...*, in *Essais*, p. 1294), with St. Augustine, *Les Confessions, trad. française d'Arnauld d'Andilly* (Paris, Garnier Frères [n.d.]), pp. 237-8.

And he took the "damnation" of unbaptized children almost as a personal affront.

His work is weakened by glaring errors and omissions. In his description of Augustine's intellectual evolution he gives undue emphasis to the "ready-made formulas" which Neoplatonism supposedly offered Augustine, whereas he says hardly a word about the literary and spiritual importance of the Bible, particularly the Gospels and the Pauline epistles. [109] It would take any Augustinian scholar a long time to find these "ready-made" Neoplatonic formulas, whereas the Scriptural quotations fill nearly every page written after Augustine's conversion. Camus' analysis of Augustine's doctrine of the Word, the Trinity, the Incarnation, and their relation to Plotinus, is especially muddled. He is incompetent in his handling of metaphysical concepts, and far more convincing when dealing with moral problems, in this essay as elsewhere.

Finally, and most significantly, Camus seems to consider the "fusion" of Hellenism and Christianity in Augustine's thought as an isolated, not to say fortuitous phenomenon, as the product of some magic coincidence. It is thanks to Augustine, he concludes, that Christianity "rose to the status of a philosophy." [110] The problem, thus stated, is excessively simplified. Augustine did not "turn Christianity into a metaphysics" any more than had Paul, Justin, Origen, Jerome, or Clement of Alexandria before him. Augustine is no more of a rationalist, no more of a metaphysician, and certainly less of a Neoplatonist, than some of his illustrious predecessors, Athanasius, for example. He did not make the mysteries of evangelical Christianity palatable to reason. What he can more accurately be said to have done was to widen the field of philosophical speculation so as to orient human reason towards problems that had previously not been considered "philosophical."

It would be pedantic in the extreme to belabor these historical points. *Christian Metaphysics* is, after all, the work of a university

---

[109] A. Camus, *Métaphysique Chrétienne...*, in *Essais*, p. 1293: "On voit donc en quel sens on peut parler d'une influence du Néoplatonisme sur la pensée chrétienne [i.e. d'Augustin] ... Elle [la pensée de Plotin] a préparé et assoupli des formules, qui en temps voulu se sont trouvées toutes faites." Camus says practically nothing of the Scriptural influences on Augustine's thought, and overstresses the importance of Neoplatonism.

[110] *Ibid.*, p. 1310.

student, and the miracle of it is that the student in question decided to embark upon such an ambitious undertaking. Whatever the shortcoming of his *diplôme*, Camus was quite certainly enriched by his readings. It is, therefore, permissible to talk of an Augustinian "influence" on Camus, though he seems to have disagreed with "that other African" on every major point. It could be that nothing in Camus would have been different had he never heard of Augustine; but I am inclined to think that Augustine served as a mirror that allowed Camus to discover those qualities that became characteristically his: the vibrant sensibility, the taste for moral issues, the conviction that any philosophical journey must begin with a withdrawal into oneself, or, as Augustine calls it, a "reditus ad intima mea" (*Confessions,* VII, 10).

CONCLUSION

The nature and content of Camus' Hellenic culture has until now remained perhaps the least explored area of his entire work, and whatever criticism has appeared has been unexceptionally encomiastic. Jacques Hardré, for example, refers to *Christian Metaphysics and Neoplatonism* as a work of "knowledge acquired by careful and thorough research."[1] Francesco Lazzari calls the essay "a richly documented, attentive and accurate piece of research."[2] Germaine Brée agrees with Henri Peyre that Greece is worthy of being called Camus' spiritual homeland, and she adds that "Camus' line of thought, like Sartre's, can be traced through Saint Augustine, Pascal, Kierkegaard, and Chestov, with Plato and the Neoplatonists as a constant check and reference."[3] Like so many general statements concerning Camus' so-called Greek line of thought, this one does not bear under the weight of critical examination. What, indeed, does it mean to "trace a *line* of thought" through thinkers whose systems are as divergent as those of Chestov and Plato? What can it possibly mean to use Plato and the Neoplatonists "as a constant check and reference"? What Neoplatonists? What check? What reference?

The purpose of my essay has evidently not been to debunk the foregoing opinions. It does seem questionable, however, whether Camus' Greek culture was either profound or accurate. His opinions on Homer, Aeschylus, Sophocles, and Plato are impressive neither for their precision nor for their critical acuity. His most memorable pages on Sisyphus

---

[1] "Camus' Thoughts on Christian Metaphysics and Neoplatonism, *"Studies in Philology,* vol. LXIV, 1967, p. 98.

[2] "Metaphysica cristiana e neoplatonismo ... , "*Revista de Studi Crociani,* April-June, 1968, pp. 234-35.

[3] Germaine Brée, *Camus* (New York, 1964), p. 25; cf. p. 21.

are almost entirely the product of schoolbook sources. His critical comments on the Presocratics, like his remarks on Greek tragedy, owe a great deal more to Nietzsche and Chestov than to the texts themselves. Whether Camus had any firsthand knowledge of Presocratic philosophy seems doubtful. His opinions on Heracleitus merely echo those of Nietzsche, which, in turn, echo those of Schopenhauer. [4] His vision of Empedocles is entirely colored by Nietzsche and Hölderlin. Not a single one of his opinions on the Presocratics would indicate that Camus knew anything about the diversity of their systems.

His acquaintance with Plotinus is not the product of a direct reading of the *Enneads*. His chapter on Neoplatonic philosophy in *Christian Metaphysics* seems to attest, as usual, to "a most learned and painful research," and to a wide acquaintance with the original text. A closer analysis of that chapter reveals, however, that Camus copied haphazardly and uncritically from the works of Emile Bréhier and René Arnou for nearly all of his opinions. An indication of Camus' rather uncritical faith in the opinions of other minds is that his attitude towards Plotinus changes entirely according to whether he is quoting Bréhier or Chestov. In *Christian Metaphysics,* he repeats Bréhier's idea that Plotinus was a tragic figure, torn between his mystical instincts and his need for rational lucidity. In *Noces* and *The Myth of Sisyphus,* on the other hand, he proposes Chestov's somewhat different thesis that Plotinus was an "intuitional" philosopher who anticipates Bergson and Husserl, and who replaces syllogistic reasoning with metaphysical insight. In neither case do Camus' opinions reflect a personal reading of the *Enneads.* I am personally inclined to discount the alleged "influence" of Plotinus on Camus and to disregard the suggestion that Plotinus had an influence on Camus' esthetics.

Camus' Greek culture, therefore, cannot be called impressive. His knowledge of Greek literature in the late thirties was that of an average, if respectable, French *licencié. Christian Metaphysics,* generally speaking, is a mediocre piece of work, though Camus made occasional use of some of his information in later years. As he grew older, however, his references to Antiquity seem to have become more accurate and more judicious. An examination of his later works bears out Jean

---

[4] Ch. Andler, *Nietzsche, sa Vie et sa Pensée,* III, p. 107, an opinion quoted in F. Nietzsche, *La Naissance de la Tragédie,* trans. by G. Bianquis, p. 8.

Grenier's remark that Greek literature continued to be a source of ever new discoveries for Camus until the end of his life. [5] There is, in any case, a marked difference between the hit-or-miss scholarship of *Christian Metaphysics* (1936), and the more precise references to Aeschylus, Epicurus, and especially Lucretius in *The Rebel* (1952). There is a marked progression from the uncritical, somewhat sophomoric repetition of Nietzsche's ideas on Greek tragedy in the *Essay on Music* (1932), and the mature lecture on *The Future of Tragedy* (1955), which, however derivative, shows signs of reflection and a fresh study of the primary sources. It should therefore be said of Camus that he never allowed himself to think he knew all there was to know about Greece. Indeed, he seems to have been more in touch with the vital sources of Greek literature after his university days than before.

He approached Greek culture with his own prejudices and preconceptions. Unlike Spinoza, he never placed understanding at the pinnacle of the mind's activity. It seemed less important to him to understand the Greek mind than to find in it an anticipation or a confirmation of his own tragic humanism. He was, naturally, correct in assuming that myths are dead objects unless the artistic imagination resurrects them; but one wonders whether it is necessary to sacrifice historical fidelity to artistic vitality. Need one necessarily choose between being a poet and a scholiast? Must Faust burn his books, or might he not be both learned and creative? Many a great modern artist has managed to combine learning with originality far better than Camus did: T. S. Eliot, Giraudoux, Gide, and Joyce, to name but a few.

According to a phrase now become fashionable with regard to Camus, he "attempted to refashion and recreate Greek thought as a revolt against the sacred." But his attitudes towards Greece, in the final analysis, reflect numerous contradictions: he seems to have read Greek literature with the expectation that it would confirm his own sense of personal revolt, yet he said of the entire body of ancient literature that it was "not a literature of dissent but of consent." He asserts that ancient myths are meaningless unless the artistic imagination can infuse new life into them, yet he consistently claims to be interpreting the Greek myths as they were intended by their authors. More generally, he asserts that the Greeks had "no sense of the supernatural," yet he spends several pages of one of his essays talking

---

[5] J. Grenier, *Albert Camus*, p. 65.

about the Greek religious mysteries. The Greeks are alleged to have made of human destiny "a man's business, which must be settled among men." Yet Aeschylus and Sophocles are referred to as admittedly religious souls; Plato and Socrates, however rational, are said to consider the material world as "a faded copy of the real;" Plotinus continuously aspires to "flee to his beloved country;" the Orphic and Eleusinian mystery cults are described as "anticipations" of Christianity.

To each of his theses on Greece, there can be found somewhere in Camus' *œuvre* a corresponding antithesis. He realized, of course, that being free of contradictions is not necessarily a mark of originality or mental vitality. But, like Nietzsche (who once quipped that even the greatest writers cannot prevent themselves from "rounding out a periodic sentence"), Camus allowed himself somewhat annoyingly to be carried away by his taste for *bel canto*, resonant generalizations, and Castillan tirades, to the point of making the Greek universe one and the same with his own. In thinking and saying, as he occasionally did, that he was going back to Greek sources after "twenty centuries of antinature and mystification," he was simply mistaken. The common ground of understanding between Camus and the Hellenic mind is, in fact, quickly covered. Most Greeks never placed absolute value in the present life; they were not opposed —quite to the contrary— to the idea of a more perfect existence in another life; they did not, *pace* Camus, consider resignation to fate as a sign of effeminacy; they did not deem immortality of the soul an improbable idea; they were not even hostile to the idea of reward and pusnishment in the netherworld....

In "Prometheus in Hell," Camus tells how, "the year the war began, I was to leave for Greece in order to retrace the voyage of Ulysses.... But I did not embark. Instead, I lined up with those who were stamping their feet in front of the gaping door of hell. Little by little we entered. At the first shriek of murdered innocence, the door slammed shut behind us. We were in hell. We have never come out." [6]

It is higly significant that history should have locked Camus out of the innocent, horizontal world of Homer, and forced him, quite despite himself, to enter the tormented, vertical world of Dante. Though he may have considered Homer's universe his spiritual homeland, history constrained him to remain in an infernal world, from which he attempted to fight his way out. Camus' spiritual odyssey, after 1939,

---

[6] "Prométhée aux Enfers," in *Essais*, p. 842.

is vertical, like Dante's, rather than circular, like Ulysses'. From *The Myth,* through *The Plague,* to *The Rebel,* there is a threefold progression of the human spirit which it is not at all exaggerated to compare with that of the *Divine Comedy.* Camus, in short, cannot be considered as a Greek, but as a modern with a Greek heart who has been compelled to face the historical paradox of Christianity.

He best described his own dilemma: "a victim of the misfortune of being born in a pagan land during Christian times." Conscious of historical Christianity, yet unable even to "imagine" the Resurrection; nostalgic for a primitive Greece, yet missing the boat that will take him to Delphi to be initiated, Camus suffered from a sense of metaphysical dispossession which I have here described neither as Greek nor as Christian, but as "Gnostic." To his entire work can perhaps be applied a curious formula with which he once summarized two centuries of Gnostic literature: "It is a Greek reflection on Christian themes." The mixture of Hellenic seed with Christian soil yielded what he himself referred to as the "wild tares of Gnosticism." [7] Like Basilides and Valentinus, those first rebels of the Christian era, Camus believed that a tragic lucidity of the spirit, in an age when faith seems impossible, is the one valid source of regeneration. What he elaborated, in a sense, was a Gnostic theory of grace.

---

[7] *Métaphysique Chrétienne et Néoplatonisme,* in *Essais,* p. 1268.